INTRODUCTION
TO THE STUDY OF THE
DIVINE COMEDY

BY

FRANCESCO FLAMINI

TRANSLATED BY

FREEMAN M. JOSSELYN

TRANSLATION REVISED AND AUGMENTED
BY THE AUTHOR

GINN AND COMPANY
BOSTON · NEW YORK · CHICAGO · LONDON

The Athenæum Press

GINN AND COMPANY · PRO-
PRIETORS · BOSTON · U.S.A.

PREFACE

This little book, although it is meant especially for young students and beginners in Dantesque studies, is not a work of compilation. I have aimed to blend in a new synthesis, with appropriate and necessary emendations, the data offered by tradition concerning the genesis of the *Commedia* and its doctrinal content, basing myself on the points which I have discussed at length in my work, now nearing its termination, *I significati reconditi della Commedia di Dante e il suo fine supremo* (" Hidden Meanings of the Divine Comedy of Dante and its Supreme End ") (Leghorn, Giusti).

I do not consider it a useless undertaking to try to restrain the interpretative caprice of the many who, without adequate preparation, entertain themselves with the symbols, the allegories, the philosophical concepts expressed or suggested in the poem. To fish up this or that concept out of the church fathers or out of the *mare magnum* of the *Summa theologica* of Aquinas, in order later to discover it in the *Commedia*, is the easiest thing in the world! Hence the wild wood of arbitrary interpretations, in which one goes astray if there be no guiding criteria. We need an organic and simple system of general interpretation, by means of which the individual allegories may cease to be susceptible of dissimilar or contradictory explanations. And I offer such an interpretation epitomized in these pages,— very far from pretending to have resolved every difficulty, but thoroughly convinced of being on the right course.

Since Dante was both orthodox and Aristotelian, it is natural that he should have followed the ethics of the Stagyrite (*his* ethics) according to the one who knew how to reconcile them so admirably with theological doctrine. Now, I have meditated over St. Thomas Aquinas's commentary on Aristotle's "Ethics," and a vivid light has come therefrom, illuminating to my eyes the sacred poem. This is the true source of the moral thought of Alighieri, abundantly put to profit in the *Convivio* as well. This is the guiding thread which should lead us in our study of the *Summa* in relation to the *Commedia*. Only by interpreting the doctrine enclosed in the letter and in the " hidden truth " of the poem according to the maxims of the Philosopher, elucidated and completed by the greatest of theologians, will it be possible for Dante students who have not a preconceived idea or the presumption to pose as innovators, to form an opinion regarding the questions which are most important for the understanding of the work, — an opinion which, like that of Aristotle and the Peripatetics, shall be "almost catholic."

This is what its readers will see attempted in this little volume, in which I have made use of every means to be clear and simple (including those of the graphic arts), even when I had to say things " hard to think on." Finally, I have added a chapter in which the fortunes of the *Commedia* are touched on, and an appendix which gives the fundamental bibliographical suggestions for the study of the poem.

FRANCESCO FLAMINI

Marina di Pisa, Italy

AUTHOR'S PREFACE TO THE TRANSLATION

The new system of Dantesque interpretation, epitomized by me in this *Avviamento allo studio della Divina Commedia* ("Introduction to the Study of the Divine Comedy"), has had a very favorable reception in the calm, judicious, impartial minds of American students. And I am very much beholden to my colleague, who, by his careful and very faithful translation (in which my thought appears at times clearer than in the original itself), has made its understanding easier and its diffusion wider among his compatriots.

The revision of the original and of the translation, which the translator and I have done together, has here and there suggested some change or correction in the text, and some additions, especially in the notes. I have also verified all the references with care, and the same may be said of the quotations from the poem, taken from the admirable translation of Norton.

In the last chapter and in the appendix I have brought the bibliography up to date, and in this the English translation is superior to the original version, and may be profitably consulted even in my own country. But especially is it my wish to be able to render some service to the compatriots of Longfellow, as well as to those of Shakespeare; so that, having overcome the grave difficulties in the way of penetrating the secret of the meanings and thoughts of Dante, the path may thereby be made plain for them to enjoy his superhumanly marvelous art.

FRANCESCO FLAMINI

PREFACE BY THE TRANSLATOR

The importance of the work of Professor Flamini as a foundation for the understanding of the Divine Comedy has suggested to the translator the desirability of presenting it to those who love and study the poem, but are without the knowledge of Italian necessary for following his exegesis in that language.

It has been translated with more attention to fidelity of rendering than to literary elegance, and the translation may be taken as faithful, since it has received the very careful revision of the author. The few notes of the translator are put in brackets. In all cases the titles have been left in their original form, as have Latin words or phrases.

In the appended bibliography the translator has added a short list of books in English, useful for the beginner in Dante study.

Thanks are due to the Houghton Mifflin Company for permission to use the late Charles Eliot Norton's admirable translations in all quotations from the *Commedia* and from the *Vita nova*. The quotations from the *Convivio* and *De monarchia* are given from the translations of Mr. Philip H. Wicksteed, and thanks are due to him and Messrs. J. M. Dent & Co. for permission to use them.

FREEMAN M. JOSSELYN

FLORENCE, ITALY

CONTENTS

A STUDY OF
THE DIVINE COMEDY

CHAPTER I

GENESIS AND PREPARATION OF THE *COMMEDIA*

1. Beatrice, woman and symbol. 2. Dante's conception of love and beauty. 3. The *Vita nova* and the *Commedia*. 4. Probable genesis of the poem. 5. Predecessors and inspirers. 6. Philosophic and theological sources of the *Commedia*.

1. Beatrice, woman and symbol. The principal aim of the "sacred poem" of Alighieri is doubtless to point out to the "deluded and ill-disposed people" [1] the way to salvation, using as an example that which, under the veil of poetic imagery, he gives us to understand happened in his own soul.

"Necessary" to salvation (as Dante himself solemnly affirms in the very important closing passage of his political treatise *De monarchia*) is the *supernatural truth revealed by the Holy Ghost by means of the prophets and hagiographers, of Jesus Christ and his disciples;* [2] that is to say, "that body of truths revealed by God to man,

---

[1] *Parad.* xxii, 39.

[2] " The truth which hence [from Heaven] rains down through Moses, through Prophets, and through Psalms, through the Gospel, and through you who wrote after the fiery Spirit made you reverend" (*Parad.* xxiv, 135–138).

" The abundant rain of the Heavenly Spirit, which is shed over the Old and over the New parchments " [testaments] (ibid. 91–93).

and which constitutes the Christian faith." This " exalts us," [1] and kindles that light without which the human intellect has not sufficient power to attain full beatitude. It is natural that this " bringer of beatitude " (*beatrice*) to man should be the " bringer of beatitude " to Dante's soul. It is natural that in the allegory of the poem (which, as we shall see, relates to us the story of the redemption and resurrection of the author's soul) the thing which, according to the imagery, leads Alighieri even to the vision of the heavenly court should be that " most truthful teaching of Christ, which is the way, the truth, and the light." [2] This it is which gives to this soul the power to rise in its speculations even to the contemplation of the loftiest truths of faith. And indeed Beatrice solemnly shows and unveils herself to Dante under the sevenfold zone of light (the seven gifts of the Holy Ghost), on the car drawn by the griffon (Jesus Christ), surrounded by the elders and by the four symbolic animals (the books of the Prophets and Hagiographers and Evangelists).

But not on this account should we deny the historical reality of " Monna Bice," [3] loved by the young Alighieri and exalted in the *Vita nova*. As we shall see, the antecedents of the imaginary action of the *Commedia* (which is the imaginary journey of Dante in flesh and blood through the realms of the dead) and those of the true action (which is the actual passage of his soul in life from misery to beatitude) unite in referring to a selfsame truth. Dante, guided in the right direction by the "youthful eyes" of Bice, is none else than Dante guided in the straight way by the earliest " demonstrations " of Revealed

---

1 *Parad.* xxii, 42.   2 *Conv.* treatise ii, chap. 9.
3 " I Lady Joan and Lady Bice see" (*Vita nova*, p. 55).

Truth. Here, that is at their source, the letter and the allegory (certainly born at the same moment in the poet's mind) have their closest relation. And in the supernatural reasoning, whereby Bice was beatrice (the bringer of beatitude), lies the ideal connection of the journey under the guidance of the one with the passage under the guidance of the other. And such reasoning is to be sought in the conception which Dante had of love and beauty, according to the spirit of the times and the doctrines followed by the poets of the "sweet new style," of whose school he was.

2. **Dante's conception of love and beauty.** The truth which we consider necessary for the soul's salvation inflames our affections with the gift of love, at the same time that it illumines the mind with the gift of wisdom, since it is bestowed upon us by the Holy Ghost.[1] And all the gifts by which the Eternal Spirit dwells within us are united in charity; and charity is especially manifested in faith working "per delectionem."[2] And so, he who turns his mind towards Revealed Truth follows the impulse of love, inspired or awakened in him through the gift of the Holy Ghost, by the pleasure taken in the beauty which accompanies it. This impulse or influx ("spiramento")[3] is the true source of poetic "inspiration,"[4] just as it is that which spiritually unites our soul

[1] The Holy Ghost is, as every one knows, the Primal Love.

[2] Cf. St. Thomas Aquinas, *Summa theologica*, pars i ii^ae, quaest. 68, art. 5; 106, art. 1; 107, art. 1; 108, art. 1.

[3] Cf. ibid. pars i, quaest. 36, art. 1.

[4] This is the true meaning of the well-known lines: "I am one who, when Love inspires me, notes, and in that mode which he dictates within, I go uttering" (*Purg.* xxiv, 52–54); lines in which many find the all too modern idea of sincerity of feeling (cf. my lecture on "Dante and the 'Sweet Style,'" in my book *Varia*, Leghorn, Giusti, 1905, pp. 8–12).

with everything that gives us true pleasure.[1] But whatever good may be found outside of the divine essence (which is the light of truth[2]) may be called "a beam of Its own radiance"[3]; hence, such is also the beauty of "lady sage" which awakens the spirit of love in gentle hearts.[4] Whence it is that when a sufficient amount of the divine light[5] appears "in the lady," love for her beauty strengthens the love which the divine light arouses, inasmuch as it holds desire fixed upon that thing which directs us to the end of true and highest good. And this is why Beatrice, when alive, led the poet in the right direction ; this is the reason for the mystic idealism with which Dante wished his lady surrounded in the amorous booklet ("libello"). For he saw the glow of truth and the fire of love radiant in her face, as they burst forth from their celestial source. Madonna Bice bore love in her eyes[6]; she resembled love to such a degree that she might have taken his name.[7] "Whenever she appeared in any place," the youthful poet tells in the *Vita nova*, "there no longer remained to me an enemy ; nay, a flame of charity possessed me, which made me pardon every one who had done me wrong ; and had any one at that time questioned me of anything, my only answer would have been 'Love,' and my face would have been clothed with humility" (chap. 11).

[1] "Love" is simply a "spiritual union of the soul and of the loved thing" (*Conv.* treatise iii, chap. 2).

[2] Cf. in various places the last canto of the *Paradiso*.

[3] *Parad.* xxvi, 31–33.

[4] *Vita nova*, sonnet "Love is but one thing with the gentle heart."

[5] Cf. *Conv.* loc. cit. ("This love, to wit the union of my soul with this gentle lady, in whom full much of the divine light was revealed to me," etc.).

[6] Sonnet xi of the *Vita nova* (p. 41).

[7] See the close of the sonnet "An amorous spirit in my heart that lay" (p. 55).

By inspiring in her " friend " this charity, in which her own goodness had its being,[1] — charity which " exemplariter " emanates from Love which is the Holy Ghost, — she directed him towards the fruition of the Highest Goodness, our final beatitude.[2]

She was, then, already his " bringer of beatitude." And not his alone ; for the " most gentle " among the gentle, who so far surpassed the other ladies,[3] exercised her beneficent force on all ; so that many, although they did not know her name, nevertheless called her " beatrice " (bringer of beatitude) because they took into account the effect she produced on them.[4] And in this they divined the truth. In a word, she was unique, on account of the divine virtue made manifest in her ; she was one of those creatures whom Aristotle calls " divine " in that famous passage on the three evil dispositions, quoted by Dante in the *Convivio* and the *De monarchia* precisely on that account. According to Alighieri, since " in the intellectual order of the universe the ascent and descent is by almost continuous steps from the lowest form to the highest and from the highest to the lowest " ; and since there is no intermediate step between the angelic nature, which is an intellectual thing, and the human soul, but " both are continuous in the order of steps " ; we must believe " that there may be

[1] All the goodness of the soul, according to St. Thomas, comes from charity. Whence it follows that it has the same amount of charity in itself as it has goodness.

[2] The good in which the elect find their satisfaction — says the poet in *Parad*. (xxvi, 16–18) — " is Alpha and Omega of every scripture that Love reads to me, either low or loud."

[3] Cf. *Purg*. xxxi, 84.

[4] It seems to me that we should thus take the much-discussed phrase " fu da molti chiamata Beatrice, li quali non sapeano che si chiamare " (*Vita nova*, chap. 2).

one so noble and of such lofty condition that he can scarce be else than an angel." Of such " condition " was Hector, of whom Homer makes Priam say that " he did not seem the son of a mortal, but of a god." And Alighieri in the *Vita nova* recalls these words quoted by Aristotle in the passage above referred to, applying them to his " very youthful angel " of such noble bearing.[1]

She was an angel then. And, withal, such that the goodness of God was received by her in the miraculous manner in which it may be received by the angels themselves, which " are without grossness of material, as though diaphanous in virtue of the purity of their form." [2] Hence, also, the peculiar quality of the corporeal beauty of Bice ; that tempered and temperate pallor ("color of love") that had reflections as of pearls,[3] because the light with which her soul was radiant shone through the diaphanous clearness of her face, as does flame through an alabaster vase. And the " true praise of God" (Beatrice) inclosed within her mortal envelope such a share of this light of truth and love (the glory of the " Sun of the Angels," [4] which penetrates the universe with its illumination) that her splendor, or " reflected light," returned up to heaven :

> An angel crieth in the mind divine,
> And saith : " O sire, on earth is to be seen
> A miracle in action, that proceeds
> From out a soul which far as here doth shine." [5]

---

[1] See *Conv.* treatise iii, chap. 7 ; *Vita nova*, ibid. The " bearing " is the " expression," in which, as well as in speech, " the divine light most freely rays " (*Conv.* ibid.).   [2] *Conv.* ibid.

[3] Color of pearls doth clothe her as doth best
Become a lady, nowise in excess.

Vita nova, p. 36.

[4] *Parad.* x, 53.   [5] *Vita nova*, p. 35.

This marvel in action, this miracle by which alone "beauty is proven," might then be called a visible argument for the glory of God ; just as her beautiful body, presenting in the highest degree the pleasures of the world,[1] suggests in itself a sort of "shade" or "vestige" of the Supreme Pleasure.[2] This is why, being turned to the miraculous lady, desire "which is a spiritual motion"[3] led Dante

> To love the Good beyond which there is nothing
> to which one may aspire.[4]

That is why any one who saw her among her companions "all welfare [salvation] hath he perfectly beheld," and why her company was for the other ladies a fair grace from heaven.[5]

3. The *Vita nova* and the *Commedia*. With these ideas in mind, the *Vita nova* may be called the vestibule of that august and solemn temple, the *Commedia*.

The *Vita nova* is the praise of the miracle ; for such was the marvelously beneficent lady, as long as she lived, as the author often affirms.[6] And in a miracle Christians

---

[1] "Never did nature or art present to thee pleasure such as the fair limbs wherein I was inclosed, and which are scattered in earth. And if the supreme pleasure thus failed thee through my death, what mortal thing should afterward have drawn thee into its desire ?" So Beatrice herself speaks to the poet (*Purg*. xxxi, 49–54).

[2] The Supreme Pleasure is God (*Parad*. xxxiii, 33).

[3] *Purg*. xviii, 31–32.   [4] *Purg*. xxxi, 22–24.

[5] *Vita nova*, sonnet xvi.

[6] "This lady [Beatrice] was accompanied by the number nine, that it might be understood that she was a nine, that is, a miracle, whose only root is the marvelous Trinity " (*Vita nova*, chap. 30). Many said, when she had passed : "This is not a woman ; rather she is one of the most beautiful angels of heaven." And others said : " She is a marvel. Blessed be the Lord who can work thus admirably " (ibid. chap. 26). "And like a thing come down, she seems to be, from heaven to earth, a miracle to show" (ibid. sonnet " So gentle and so gracious "). Love looks at her, and " to himself he swears that God in her a new thing means to make " (Ode " Ladies that have," p. 36).

recognized a material attestation of Eternal Truth.[1]   The
Commedia is the glorification of the truth itself, as attested
by the miracle — that is, of the Eternal Truth as revealed
to us.   And in this latter, bestowed upon us by the Primal
Love through the Supreme Wisdom, Dante indicates to
us our beatitude (beatrice).   In the *Vita nova* we are told
of the manner in which the interior beauty of Beatrice,
during her life,[2] operated beneficently on the poet through
her eyes ("balconies" of the soul),[3] and through the
mouth (where the light which exists within coruscates in a
smile),[4] making him mount toward the " good of the intellect " by the true way, far from the false images of good.[5]
In the *Commedia* we are told, under the veil of that *poetic
imagery*, which we shall treat of later, how that very beauty,
that " splendor of living light eternal," [6] has illuminated
with a ray the poet's soul which, after the death of his
beatitude (beatrice), had gone astray in pursuit of the
deceitful " present things " ; [7] how that very beauty has
restored to the poet's soul the full and right use of his

[1] The chiefest foundation of our faith are " the miracles wrought by
him who was crucified, and wrought afterwards in his name by his
saints " (*Conv.* treatise iii, chap. 7).   Whereby we may apply to the
material Beatrice all that Alighieri, explaining the literal sense of
the ode " Love that discourses to me in my mind," says of the " miraculous lady of power " there eulogized.   " Inasmuch as many are so
stubborn as to doubt of these miracles (of Christ and of the Saints)
[because of some cloud], [and can] not believe any miracle unless they
have [visible] experience of the same ; and inasmuch as this lady is a
thing visibly miraculous, whereof the eyes of men may take daily
experience, and which may assure us of the possibility of the others, it
is manifest that this lady with her wondrous aspect ' aideth our faith.' "
So, too, Beatrice, like this lady, " from eternity " was ordained in the
mind of God " in testimony of the faith to those who live in these
times " (ibid.).

[2] Cf. *Vita nova*, chaps. 10 and 11.   [5] See *Purg.* xxx, 121–123.
[3] *Conv.* treatise iii, chap. 8.   [6] *Purg.* xxxi, 139.
[4] Ibid.   [7] Ibid. 34–36.

reason ; how it has redeemed him from the slavery of sin ; how it has brought it to pass that he, having explored to the depths the " way not true " upon which he had started, and having turned anew to the straight road, has mounted — becoming righteous step by step — to the " blessedness of this life, which consists in the exercise of his proper power, and is figured by the Terrestrial Paradise ";[1] and, finally, how it has revealed itself to him — satisfying the " ten years' thirst " of its faithful one [2] — far more radiant than before, since the envelope of the flesh no longer hides the divine essence.

This scene of revelation is the culminating point of the narration. When, at last, the so longed-for " beautiful eyes " of the bringer of beatitude of his youthful years are again turned on Dante (as well as the mouth, until then veiled) ; then the "eternal light," the divine light of truth, reflected from the Word (the griffon) in the mirror of her eyes and of her " holy smile," bursts forth from every veil, spreading itself through the open air, and enwraps the poet, irradiates him, dazzles him. Who can describe it ? Only the harmony of the whirling spheres can give us a " shadow," a pale counterfeit of that stupendous reflection, that light of beauty which is, at the same time, both truth and love :

O splendor of living light eternal![3] Who has become so pallid under the shadow of Parnassus, or has so drunk at its cistern, that he would not seem to have his mind encumbered, trying to render

---

[1] According to the close of the *De monarchia*, which we shall often have occasion to quote.

[2] Cf. *Purg.* xxxii, 1–3.

[3] *Splendor* is the light which is thrown back by the " part which it illuminates " (*Conv.* treatise iii, chap. 14). Such is that light which reached Dante from Beatrice ; since the Eternal Pleasure which was

thee as thou didst appear there where with its harmony the heaven [gives a mere shadow of thy beauty], when in the open air thou didst [burst forth]?[1]

By means of this ever-increasing "splendor," the eyes and the smile of the lady who celebrates her triumph in the Earthly Paradise (in other words, her *demonstrations* and her *persuasions*) [2] will lead Dante even to the fruition of the Primal Truth and Primal Good, the goal of the understanding and affections. Thus, spiritually, he will be exalted to that godlike kingdom of pure light full of love, in which our concreate "thirst" is appeased.

4. Probable genesis of the poem. Why, then, does Dante in the *Commedia* represent that the beautiful Florentine, who, as related in the *Vita nova*, with marvelous aspect guided the poet toward the beatitude of this world and that of the other, — why does he represent that, after having risen from flesh to spirit, she procures for him the means of visiting in succession the Earthly and the Celestial Paradise, which symbolize this twofold beatitude? Because by this he wishes to give us to understand that the same supernatural light, enamoring him by its beauty in the "new life" [3] (that is, in his youth), shone from the countenance of Monna Bice for his salvation; and that, after a ten years' moral wandering, this light procured for him the possibility of tasting successively the happiness of acting according to virtue, and contemplating the lofty

illuminating her directly, " from her fair face" contented the poet " with its second aspect " * (cf. *Parad.* xviii, 16–18). To this *reflection* of the eternal light does the poet turn here — not to the literal Beatrice, a mere *reflector* of this splendor.

[1] *Purg.* xxxi, 139–145.
[2] Cf. *Conv.* treatise iii, chap. 15.   [3] Cf. *Purg.* xxx, 115.

* " Its aspect reflected from the eyes of Beatrice " (Norton).

mysteries of faith. And this was accomplished by inducing him to become righteous and holy, first, through her manifestation of herself to his mind as the bringer of beatitude to human kind [1] (appearance of Beatrice to Vergil in Limbo) ; later by revealing herself to him as a reflection of the " true light " of the Word (triumph of Beatrice in the Earthly Paradise) ; and finally by her appearance as an inseparable companion of the one who impersonates contemplative life (glorification of Beatrice beside Rachel in the Celestial Paradise).

In this progressive revelation, to the mental eyes of the poet, of the glory of " that blessed Beatrice (bringer of beatitude) who liveth in heaven with the angels and on earth with my soul," [2] we should recognize the concept around which was formed that design of a pilgrimage through the three ultramundane realms, which Dante has drawn so wonderfully in his *Commedia*.

A few years, indeed, after the death of his Bice, Dante's thoughts, impelled by Love, mounted to the Empyrean and distinguished there, by the splendor which she shed, his lady, such in appearance that the mind could not comprehend her.[3] Whereupon he had a " wonderful vision " ; " in which I saw things," he writes, " which made me resolve to speak no more of this blessed one until I could

---

[1] Right reason (Vergil) shows him this by calling Beatrice " the lady that alone has power to cause men to transcend, by exalting themselves, all that is under the moon, that is, in the world " (" O Lady of Virtue! through whom alone the human race excels [passes beyond] all contained within that heaven which has the smallest circles."—*Inf*. ii, 76–78).

[2] *Conv*. treatise ii, chap. 2.

[3] He sees her such that his reporting words
To me are dark, his speech so subtile is
Unto the grieving heart which makes him tell.

Vita nova, sonnet " Beyond the sphere," etc., p. 89.

more worthily *treat* of her." [1] This *treatment*, by means of which the poet hoped to say of her "what was never said of any woman," cannot be other than the *Commedia ;* that is, the poem in which — as is announced in the proposition or exposition of the subject made in the verses

> But in order to treat of the good that I found in it,
> I will tell of the other things that I saw there —

the salvation of the soul is *treated* of, that salvation that Dante, guided in pursuit of it by Vergil, goes on acquiring as he journeys. It is indeed Beatrice who secures it for him through her sending of Vergil ; it is indeed Beatrice who later makes him mount even to the fruition of that good in which the Ultimate Salvation consists.

To confound such a *treatment* with the wonderful vision in which it had its origin, is to confound cause and effect. If the effect was the *Commedia*, then the cause will be the primitive idea of the Dantesque masterpiece. And this is in nowise the description and narration of a dream,[2] but an imaginary allegorical account of a journey which, for a most lofty end, God granted Dante to make in the ultramundane realms, as was once granted to Æneas and afterwards to St. Paul. In this great work there is, none the less, a very real vision : the ecstatic vision of the heavenly court and of its ruler, which, thanks to St. Bernard, is vouchsafed the poet, who is "held in slumber"— that is to say, that he is mentally awake, while his physical senses are in a torpor.[3] After having conducted him

---

[1] Last chapter of the *Vita nova*, which begins, "After this sonnet a wonderful vision appeared to me," etc.

[2] See my *Significati* (cited in the Preface), part i, chap. 2.

[3] " But because the time flies which holds thee slumbering " (*Parad.* xxxii, 139). In this verse St. Bernard merely refers to the state in which Dante is during the ecstatic vision which he obtains for Dante.

to the point where he could look upon the *general* structure of Paradise, Beatrice goes and takes her place in the
seat which is awaiting her beside Rachel. She who makes
blessed has fulfilled her task. To know *in detail* the court
of heaven, " to fix the look through the eternal light,"
demands more " abundant sight," demands the grace of
spiritual rapture. And it is, indeed, while in this rapture
that the poet, pointed to it by St. Bernard, the symbol of
the habit of Contemplation, sees the true glory of Beatrice
seated " with the ancient Rachel."

Now what else can the wonderful vision be, through
which Dante was induced to write the *Commedia*, than the
very vision with which it ends, and to which the magnificent "treatment" is ordered and subordinated ? Since his
thought was exalted to the Empyrean, and had become aware
that Beatrice was there " by her splendor" (as we read in
the last sonnet of the *Vita nova*, and in the prose attached
thereto), what other wonderful thing could Dante see in his
lady but " the quality of her " — that quality which he had
not understood (so subtle was its speech) when his thought
reported it to him after it had returned from on high ?
Imagination has brought the poet to her in spirit ; ecstasy,
the result of the habit of contemplation (St. Bernard),
reveals her essence to him. Even in this very vision
Beatrice, the companion of her (Rachel) who symbolizes
Contemplative Life, will have appeared to the ecstatic eyes
of her lover as the most exalted symbol of Revealed Truth.

And so we see maturing in his mind this double concept of a vast poem. On the one hand, Supernatural
Truth, as revealed to us, twice triumphing in the person
of his dead lady : once on earth, in the peace of Eden
(which symbolizes the happiness of the active life) on the

car of the Church, which dispenses to mortals her inesti-
mable benefits ; and secondly in heaven, in the radiance of
the Empyrean (which symbolizes the happiness of the
contemplative life). And on the other hand, himself, the
poet, in a visionary journey, raised by his enduring love
for his lady from the baseness of a valley of misery [1] to
the height of a hill of joy ; [2] and then guided by her even
to the Empyrean ; and finally, while still alive, admitted
by her intercession to the beatitude of the sight of God.

Thus to identify the dead loved one with the bringer of
beatitude to the entire human race is truly to say of her
what was never said of any woman ! To sing of this double
apotheosis of Revelation, a subject most fitting to the matter
and to the end of a poem in which heaven and earth have
collaborated ; to represent under poetic imagery the redemption of man, as it was accomplished by the Word in
the fullness of time, and as the longed-for return of the
" good world " will again obtain it for us from God ; truly
that is to treat worthily of her !

5. Predecessors and inspirers of Dante. The idea of
coloring this sketch by means of the narration of a visit
made by him to the otherworld might have been suggested
to Dante by the knowledge (which we may fairly suppose
that he possessed) of that considerable cycle of legends on
the destiny of man after death, which, in the Middle Ages,
were inspired by the religious ardor which populated the
hermitages of the Thebaid and the monasteries of the
West. At the beginning, these legends aimed merely to
soften harsh and ferocious spirits by the terror of future

---

[1] The valley which contains the " dark wood " (*Inf.* i, 2 and 14).
[2] The mountain of the Earthly Paradise, on the slopes of which
Dante has placed Purgatory.

torments ; hence their childish ingenuousness and very simple mechanism. But if the ingenuousness remained, the mechanism increased little by little in richness and complexity. Thus we have the " Vision of St. Paul," those legends which have come to us from the cloisters of far-off Ireland (the "Voyage of St. Brandan," the "Vision of Tungdalus," the " Purgatory of St. Patrick "), and finally the " Vision of Frate Alberico," a monk of Monte Cassino who lived in the twelfth century. All of these contain pictures akin to those in the poem of Dante ; as the Lucifer of the legend of Tungdalus who crunches and devours the souls, or the devils in the legend of Alberico who try to catch with grappling irons the author who has been left alone a moment by his guide. But in treating an argument of this sort concerning the lot of the good and evil souls, which the populace liked to see represented on the walls of churches and cemeteries, put on the stage in the popular plays, and reproduced in the town squares by the public reciters in their ballads, Dante brought order, symmetry, unity of conception, and poetic mastery, where there had been merely a disordered mass of extravagant or frightful incidents. He brought into the realms of the infinite and the divine the consideration of the things of this world, with the intention — supreme aim of the " sacred poem " — of removing mankind from the state of misery and of directing it to the state of happiness. In the hands of the glorious artificer the rough monastic odysseys were transformed into a journey through the realms of punishment, purification, and reward, constructed with all the rigor of science. And the *Commedia*,[1] which

---

[1] This title is the antithesis of *tragedía* given by Alighieri himself (*Inf.* xx, 113) to the "Æneid." Dante wrote and pronounced *Comedía*.

describes this journey (so called by reason of the material which is not always lofty, and of the consequent choice of language which is not always overnice), is structurally well proportioned, symmetrical, and almost mathematical. It has three parts (Hell, Purgatory, and Paradise, all ending with the word " stars ") of thirty-three cantos each, except that the first part has one more, which serves as a general introduction. There are, then, one hundred cantos, in which the numbers three and nine (which is a multiple of three) dominate, and even the meter is in stanzas of three lines bound together by their rhymes,[1] that is, by " terzine."

Far different, moreover, from the wretched precursors which we have just indicated, were the inspirers of this marvelous work of art. Dante had before him an immense repertory of images and of symbolic figures, a vast treasure house of conceptions well adapted to poetic treatment : the Bible. This book and its numerous commentators (among whom St. Thomas Aquinas is especially to be noted) often give us the clue to the secrets of such a work as the *Commedia*, which has, in common with the Sacred Scriptures, profound allegory and loftiness of purpose, as well as narrative and, at times, didactic and exhortatory form. The writers of classic antiquity also stimulated the imagination of Alighieri and trained his execution to no small degree. It is true, indeed, that the poet (since he did not know Greek) was acquainted with the Greek writers only through translations or quotations found in the Latin classics, in the church fathers, in anthologies, and in encyclopedic lexicons. On the other hand, he was

[1] Metrical scheme : ABA . BCB . CDC . DED . . . XYX . Y. In Italy the joining of the stanzas by rhyme is characteristic of the " serventese " (a common form of poetic composition).

thoroughly familiar with the best Latin writers (although he did not always interpret them precisely[1]) ; he knew the whole of Vergil's "Æneid" by heart.[2]　Indeed, he declared that he had taken from the "Æneid" the style which he did not hesitate to call " fair," and which, even before the composition of the *Commedia*, had " done him honor " [3] in the lyric poems which circulated "among the people." It was from the masterpiece of Vergil that he had gained that clearness and preciseness of form that his tremendous genius enabled him to carry out to wonderful perfection. From the same work (notably in the sixth book, where the descent of Æneas to the realm of the dead is described) have come to him ideas and expressions which show the marks of their origin, even through his free and artistic treatment of them.

Besides the "Æneid" it is proved that Dante knew the " Bucolics " (but not the " Georgics," although it would be hardly prudent categorically to deny him any knowledge of them).　It is also known that he was familiar with the satires of Juvenal, the *Poetica* of Horace, the *Pharsalia* of Lucan, the *Thebais* of Statius, and especially the *Metamorphoses* of Ovid.　There are evident from time to time throughout the three parts of the *Commedia* reminiscences of these works, if not imitations.　And even where our master poet remodels both fact and thought, we not infrequently feel in the turn of a phrase, in the coloring of a picture, in the quality of a comparison, the skillfully handled influence of the great art of the classic writers.

---

[1] In the *Conv.* (treatise ii, chap. 6) he is incorrect in his interpretation of verses 664–665 of the first book of the "Æneid."　In *Purg.* (xxii, 40) Dante failed to understand the famous phrase " Quid non mortalia pectora cogis Auri sacra fames ? " ("Æneid," iii, 56–57).

[2] Cf. *Inf.* xx, 114.　　　　　　　　[3] Cf. *Inf.* i, 82–87.

6. Philosophic and theological sources of the *Commedia*.
But the masterpiece of Dante, in the intention of the author,
is a work of science, no less than a work of art. And its
teaching, which flows copiously both from the truth hidden
under the poetic imagery and from the vast doctrinal element, which is truth and not imagery, has a thoroughly
philosophic character. From what sources did Dante
obtain this? What books determined the direction and
the nature of his thought?

Dante was of the school of Aristotle. The "master of
those that know"[1] was for him the supreme authority
in philosophical questions.[2] We find the "Nicomachean
Ethics" called "the ethics of Dante himself" (that is to
say, the ethics which the latter, by following exactly, has
made his own) in a passage from the *Inferno*[3] which is most
important for the determination of the fundamental philosophic source of a poem such as the *Commedia*, whose
content is almost entirely ethical. Dante was not familiar
with the original text (for we know that he did not read
Greek), but he did know the two Latin versions, which he
cites in a very well-known passage in the *Convivio* (treatise ii,
chap. 15); and especially that version which Thomas Aquinas directed and on which he actually worked, which was
based on the Greek text and not on the Arabic translation.

We must then read and meditate upon the "Ethics" of
the Stagyrite in the version consecrated by the authority
of Aquinas, if we wish to determine the moral content of

---

1 *Inf.* iv, 131. Elsewhere Dante calls him "master of the philosophers" (*Conv.* treatise iv, chap. 8), "magister sapientum" (*De vulgari
eloquentia*, book ii, chap. 10).

2 "Wherever the divine opinion of Aristotle has opened its mouth,
methinks that every other's opinion may be dropped" (*Conv.* treatise
iv, chap. 17).   3 xi, 80.

the *Inferno* and *Purgatorio* presented under the form of a poem.[1] And not this work alone, but also the considerable commentary that St. Thomas himself wrote upon it[2] and which we find cited and largely drawn upon in the *Convivio*. For Dante, at the same time a fervent Aristotelian and rigorous in his orthodoxy, was, as is natural, a follower of St. Thomas, whose merit as a philosopher consists in having reconciled in a masterly manner the church doctrines with those of Aristotle and of his Arabian commentators. In his *Summa theologica*, while propounding the truths of Revelation, he reasons keenly upon and discusses those of natural speculation, which were at that time based almost entirely on the authority of the Stagyrite. Hence, even more than the *Summa catholicae fidei contra Gentiles*, which Alighieri cites not infrequently in the *Convivio*, this *Summa theologica*, which he does not cite but whose ideas he often repeats integrally, may be considered as a very considerable source of the doctrine inclosed in the *Commedia*, both manifest and hidden. The poet has chosen two saints to demonstrate and to illustrate the "fourth family of the exalted Father, who always satisfies it, showing how He breathes forth, and how He begets"; and Thomas Aquinas is the one he follows as guide in the theological-philosophical conception of his immortal work.[3]

[1] Aristotle is called the "praeceptor morum" in the *De monarchia*, treatise iii, chap. 1. "Ut refert Philosophus in iis quae de moribus fugiendis ad Nicomachum," as we read in the same work (ii, 3).

[2] *Sancti Thomae Aquinatis praeclarissima commentaria in decem libros ethicorum Aristotelis* (operum vol. v), Paris, 1660.

[3] Of the other works of St. Thomas, Dante might also have known his commentary to that famous *Liber sententiarum* which was the textbook of theological instruction in all the schools in Christendom. The *Commedia* is in some degree indebted to this book and to its author, Peter Lombard, who originated that school of which the great Aquinas was a leader (as well as to Albertus Magnus, St. Thomas's master).

But this does not exclude the possibility that the other of these two saints, Bonaventura da Bagnorea, might have suggested to Alighieri some part of his conception. It merely excludes the possibility that the poet, whose extremely close relationship to Aquinas is proven even to the point of the use of identical forms of logical and dialectic processes, could have belonged, or shows that he did belong, to the "mystic and Augustinian current." For, if the "Confessions" and *De civitate Dei* were familiar to him, and if he certainly knew some of the writings of St. Bonaventura (as well as those of St. Bernard and other fathers and doctors), the fulcrum of his entire philosophical and theological system is composed of the two *Summae* and the commentaries to Aristotle by Thomas Aquinas. Some ideas, besides, came to him from *De officiis* and from *De finibus bonorum et malorum* of Cicero, and still more (many more) from the *Philosophiae consolatio* of Boetius. And it was in reading these authors, as he affirms in the *Convivio*, that he was initiated into the secrets of philosophy.[1]

---

[1] Cf. *Conv.* treatise ii, chap. 13.

CHAPTER II

NATURE AND MEANING OF THE POEM

1. Poetry and its aims according to the mediæval view. 2. The *Commedia* is a didactic and allegorical poem. 3. What senses Dante distinguished in the interpretation of literary compositions. 4. The senses of the *Commedia*: the allegory and the anagoge.[1]

1. Poetry and its aims according to the mediæval view. The poem of Dante corresponds perfectly to the philosophic and religious ideals of the times in which it was written; for the Middle Ages live again in it, with their peculiar ideas, their symbolism, and their allegory.

What impression did the *Commedia* make on its earliest readers? "Most subtle," and written "for the good of all," we reply with Guido da Pisa and Graziolo Bambaglioli. Fit to draw mortals upward toward the highest forms of human knowledge, thanks to the extraordinary privilege granted its author by God, who "filled him with His spirit." Alighieri was hailed by the generation immediately following his death as a philosopher and theologian, as well as a poet, and the *Commedia* seemed a miracle of science rather than a masterpiece of art. Moreover, he himself, after he had sung the mysteries of Faith, believed himself more worthy of the eagerly desired laurel because he had become a poet "with other voice and with other fleece,"[2] that is, poet-theologian.

---

[1] [Anagoge may be taken to mean "spiritual sense."]
[2] See *Parad.* xxv, 1-12.

Let us see what idea of the character, of the ends, and of the aims of poetry (and of the art of the use of words, in general) was held in the Middle Ages and by Dante.

Since the outbursts of sentiment and the conceptions of the imagination were all directed to God and the second life, the men of the Middle Ages considered poetic art simply as a means whereby to ennoble and sanctify the spirit, in preparation for its spiritual end. Wherefore the imaginings of the classic poets were either condemned as false and corrupting, or considered to have meanings which were never dreamed of by their authors. And the new poetry was appreciated, not according to æsthetic standards, but according to its greater or less educational value and its more or less rich ethical content. To instruct while pleasing — that was the true end of poetry in the eyes of the men of the Middle Ages. Vergil was as much admired as a philosopher, who proclaimed under the veil of his imaginings teachings useful for the moral conduct of man, as he was as a worthy master of poetic art. And every poet ought to have regard for such conduct, if he did not wish his work to be in vain, for beauty was sought for in the degree in which it could attract man to the intellectual fruition of truth. Poetry was reverenced as a noble lady, with the understanding that she should remain a vassal to the two powerful queens, Theology and Philosophy. Boccaccio, in a long digression about poetry interpolated in his *Vita di Dante*,[1] affirms that the ancient poets followed in the footsteps of the Holy Ghost, who revealed His secrets to future generations through the words of many, " making them say in word under a veil that which, in due time, He intended to show unveiled in act "; and

[1] Edition Macrí-Leone, Florence, Sansoni, 1888, pp. 48–56.

that the poetic fables were devised in order that their beauty might attract "those whom neither the demonstrations nor the persuasions of philosophy had been able to draw to themselves." He concludes that theology and poetry are practically the same thing![1]

2. The *Commedia* is a didactic and allegorical poem. Dante in this respect (as in so many other things) does not depart from the ideas of his time. For him, that poetry which is outwardly beautiful, while inwardly empty of all noble and lofty ideas, is like an ugly woman clothed in

[1] This is the same conclusion which Petrarch reached in one of his letters to his brother Gerard, December 2, 1348 (*Fam.* lib. x, epistola 4, ed. Fracassetti, ii, 82). In this he says : " Poetry is in nowise contrary to theology. You are amazed ? I am almost inclined to say that theology is the poetry of God. To say that Christ is now a lion, now a lamb, now a worm, what is this but poetry ? You will find a thousand phrases like these in Scripture ; it would take too long to quote more. What else do the words of the Savior in the Evangel signify, if not a discourse different from the apparent meaning, that is, to use a single word, *alieniloquium*, which we call in more usual terms, *allegory ?* And so, all poetry is embroidered with discourses of this kind. But the subject matter is different. Who can deny it ? In theology the subject matter is God and divine things, in poetry, gods and men. Whence, even in Aristotle, we read, 'the first theologians were poets.'"

Boccaccio says the same things in the notable ending of the abovementioned digression : "I say that theology and poetry can be considered as almost one and the same thing when their subject is the same. Indeed I go further and assert that theology is simply the poetry of God. What is it but a poetic fiction to say in one place of Scripture that Christ is a lion and in another a lamb, now that He is a serpent and now a dragon, and in still another place that He is a rock ? And He is called by many other names, to repeat all of which would take too long. What else signify the words of the Savior in the Gospel, if not a teaching different from the outward sense, which manner of speaking we term, using a more common word, *allegory ?* It is clear, then, that not only is poetry theology, but also that theology is poetry. And truly if my words, in so great a matter, merit little credence, I shall not be disturbed ; at least let Aristotle, a most worthy authority on all great questions, be believed, who affirmed that he found the poets were the first theologians " (J. R. Smith, " Earliest Lives of Dante," Holt & Co.).

silk and jewels.[1] Erudition is required of a poet, no less
than intellect. And in the measure that, of the three parts
of the human soul (animal, vegetable, and rational), the
latter is exalted above the others, just so much will that
virtue, which is its object, be the object of the highest form
of poetry ;[2] hence the moral purpose which Dante considered necessary for this form, and his resolute attitude
as the poet of righteousness. The right direction of the
will (*directio voluntatis*), necessary to the attainment of
true virtue,[3] is the principal care of the author of the
Commedia in the "long way" from the wood to the
Celestial Jerusalem. In the poem, upon which he spent
all the force of his intellect for many years, Alighieri
meant to teach — as he considered the office of true poetry
— the moral way to happiness in this world and the next.

Dante's masterpiece is, then, essentially didactic, — a
work of art, to be sure, but at the same time scientific.
Didactic, and consequently allegorical ; just as he considered the "Æneid" to be, — that book in which he recognized a treasure house of wisdom under a poetic covering.
The moral and religious teaching of the *Commedia* is not
developed wholly in the letter, that is, in the literal sense.
Beside the frankly doctrinal part, which consists in the
teachings enounced from time to time to the author by his
guides and the spirits with whom he has to do, — to say
nothing of the digressions and invectives in which he himself indulges, — there is another and much broader part.
And the didactic content of this latter is to be sought
under the veil of that imaginary action which constitutes
the letter of the poem. Dante himself in two places in

---

[1] *De vulgari eloquentia*, ed. Rajna, pp. 112–113.
[2] Ibid. pp. 112, 118–120.   [3] Cf. ibid. p. 120.

his work [1] invites his readers to sharpen their eyes to the *truth* which is under the *veil*. And in both places the doctrine emerges, not from what is pictured there, but from the truth veiled by the imagery, that is to say, from the allegorical sense; for the latter is none else than (to use his own words) "a truth hidden under beauteous fiction." [2]

In fine, Dante intended to give to his fellow countrymen a didactic-allegorical poem, like the *Roman de la Rose* or the *Tesoretto* of Brunetto Latini. And, with this in view, if he succeeded in producing a very different and infinitely better work of art, that should not make us forget what he intended his book to be in its essence. Not without good reason did his sons and the other earliest commentators of the "lofty Comedy" pay particular attention to bringing to light the treasures of doctrine inclosed in the envelope of his poetic imaginings. Only by studying the hidden meanings of the *Commedia* can one come fully to penetrate the aims of the author, to discover in them the influence of the spirit of the times, to determine exactly the supreme end at which he aimed in his poetry.

3. What senses Dante distinguished in the interpretation of literary compositions. But to trace out these meanings we must know what senses Dante distinguished in the interpretation of literary compositions.

For that he made such distinctions in his interpretation, following the generally accepted principles for biblical exegesis as the basis for every line of thought in this connection, hardly admits of doubt. The Word of God closed the treasure house of wisdom, and he who wished, as did Dante, to provide the reader with "life-giving nourishment"

---

[1] *Purg.* viii, 19–21 ; *Inf.* ix, 61–63.
[2] *Conv.* treatise ii, chap. 1.

by the same means, must follow its methods and procedure. Now, according to Thomas Aquinas,[1] in the Scriptures we are to look for four meanings: the *historic*, or *literal*, and three "spiritual" senses, which are based upon this latter and presuppose it, that is, the *allegorical*, the *moral*, and the *anagogic*. The literal sense is found in the natural meaning of the words of the text; the other senses, not in the words themselves, but in the signification given to the things which these words indicate. Upon the first of these spiritual senses the other two depend, and from it they are derived. We must pass from the literal to the allegorical meaning; from the latter, then, we deduce the moral and the anagogic, bearing always in mind that the first ought to teach us what we must do, and that the other has reference to the things of eternal glory.

This is all that Alighieri could extract from his master about the senses to be enclosed in his *Commedia*, when he was thinking it out. For St. Thomas allowed him full liberty regarding what he was to understand by the allegorical sense (and, consequently, what he was to take as his point of departure for the other two spiritual senses). Now what was Dante's attitude in this, starting from the distinctions laid down by Aquinas?

The " Epistle to Cangrande," although it pretends to be an introduction to the whole poem,[2] gives us no light on this point. Its author — whether it be Dante or (as is more probable) a rhetorician imitating his Latin style — at first merely adapts St. Thomas's theory to a certain

---

[1] *Summa theologica*, pars 1, quaest. 1, art. 10; pars 1 ii[ae], quaest. 102, art. 2.

[2] [Professedly] composed upon offering the third " cantica " to Cane della Scala, together with a detailed commentary on its " prologue," that is, upon the first twelve " terzine."

example taken from the stories in the Old Testament, which is not relevant for the interpretation of an imaginary action, such as the letter of the *Commedia*. Afterwards he indicates an allegorical sense for the scene of this action, which is the state of souls after death, but not for the action itself, which is the poet's imaginary journey "among the dead people."

Fortunately the way to follow for the understanding of the meaning of this journey (hence also of the guides, the aids, the hindrances, which are found in it) is indicated to us by a thoroughly authenticated work, most valuable for the knowledge of Dante's philosophical ideas. In the *Convivio*[1] we find not only a long exposition of Alighieri's idea of the senses of the Scriptures, with apt examples, but also an application of these senses themselves (as he, a poet, conceived them) to a work of lofty poetry and auto-biographical imagery. For such was, indeed, the *Convivio*, and hence it did not differ in many respects from his *Commedia*. From it we find : (1) that it was Dante's idea, as well as that of St. Thomas, that the Scriptures ought to be " chiefly " expounded in four senses, — the *literal*, the *allegorical*, the *moral*, and the *anagogic ;* (2) that the allegorical sense "after the use of the poets " (Dante's meaning here is "to follow the method of the poets") may be defined as "a truth hidden under beauteous fiction," since the literal sense (the "literal story") is imagery,[2] when treating of poetry ; (3) that the moral sense is that which every reader ought " to go intently noting " in literary

---

[1] Treatise ii, chap. 1.

[2] The allegorical sense of a poetic composition is, then, according to Alighieri, that story or that affirmation of a truth, whatever it may be, which the author has embellished, hiding it under the veil of ingeniously constructed imagery.

compositions, in order to extract therefrom teachings for the conduct of their lives; [1] (4) that the anagogic sense, or "supersense," consists in a truth which is the raising of another truth to a meaning having reference "to eternal glory."

In applying such a theory of the senses of poetic compositions to the "exposition" of the first two odes of the *Convivio*, Alighieri is almost completely silent as to the anagogic and moral senses.[2] But he offers us a valuable example of how we are to pass from the veil of a poetic image to the underlying truth, that is, to the *allegorical sense* (from which spring the anagoge and the morality). He tells us that what he recounts about himself in those odes is an invention meant to symbolize that which happened in his soul. In them he has imagined his *love for a lady*, which shall signify his actual *ardor for philosophy*.

4. The senses of the *Commedia*: the allegory and the anagoge. And so in his poem Dante has hidden truth and doctrine under the mantle of autobiographic imagery and a lady's glorification. So, too, in it he has introduced himself as the protagonist of the story.

The *Commedia* in its literal sense is, throughout, a narration of events which happened to its author. Nevertheless, we must distinguish the antecedents of the action from the action itself. The latter, the journey through the ultramundane realms, is poetic imagery; the former, the straying of Dante,[3] are (or aim to be) a truth in narrative form expressed by means of "some figure or rhetorical coloring."[4]

---

[1] This is, as well, the teaching that buds forth from the "hidden truth," that is, from the *allegorical sense.*

[2] For the cause of this silence, see my *Significati*, i, 46–47.

[3] See *Inf.* i, 1–30; *Purg.* xxx, 103–145; xxxi, 22–60; xxxiii, 85–90.

[4] See *Vita nova*, chap. 25.

These actual antecedents ally themselves easily and completely with the " allegorical and true " action, which is indicated by the letter and imagery, that is, by the aforesaid imaginary journey; if, in accord with some of the earliest commentators, we suppose Dante himself to be the "agent" of the allegorical action as well as of the imaginary.[1] By this is meant : if we consider that this allegory consists in the actual passing of the poet's soul, while alive, from the state of unhappiness and abjection caused by his straying (the " valley " of the first canto), first, to the state of blessedness which the exercise of our own virtue procures for us (the table-land of the Earthly Paradise), then to that transitory state of the beatific vision seen in a spiritual ecstasy and obtained by the Divine Goodness.[2]

If we take the allegory of the poem in this way, we draw from it a complete narration of what it pleases Dante to have us believe took place in his mind up to the completion of his own intellectual and moral regeneration. And it is very clear that this allegory is to be sought only and always in the part of the work where there is poetic imagery ; that is to say, in the author's " fated going," and consequently in the regions through which he professes he passed, in the guides, the aids, and the hindrances relative to this journey. And it is likewise clear that the literal sense (from which we should always start) ought to be carefully distinguished from the allegorical, since each

[1] This is what happens, both as regards the imaginary and the allegorical action, in the two odes of the *Convivio* already cited, which Dante himself shows us how to interpret.

[2] The real action will have reference, then, to the incorruptible part of Dante, in as far as this, united with the corruptible, tends toward the two ends which Providence has laid out for man, *prout corruptibilis* and *prout incorruptibilis*, and attains these in the measure possible in this world. See *De monarchia*, treatise iii, chap. 16.

represents an action complete in itself, which begins, continues, and ends without commingling.

As regards the anagogic sense, which is a truth superposed upon another truth by which it is symbolized, in the
Commedia this ought to spring forth not from the letter
(which is imagery) but from the allegory (which is truth).
The true narration of Dante's salvation (or of the passing
of his soul from the unhappiness, caused by his straying,
to the two states of happiness above pointed out) will be
the narration of the redemption of man (or of the passing
of the human soul from the unhappiness in which it lay
for " many centuries," caused by the first sin, to the two
states of happiness proper to this world and the other,
and which were reopened when in the fullness of time
" it pleased the Word of God to descend ").[1]

And this is anagoge in its highest form ; for Alighieri
could, in his *Commedia*, signify no other fact having reference to the " supernal things of eternal glory," which could
be more sublime than the exit of the soul from sin, than
its restitution to that glory, than its sanctification through
the works of Jesus Christ.[2]

There are, then, two truths, the *allegorical* and the
anagogic, which we must uncover from under the veil of
the imagery.[3] The action of the poem is threefold (as are
so many other things in it !) : the *literal* or " imaginary,"
the *allegorical* or " true," the *anagogic* or " superposed."

[1] See *Parad*. vii, 26–30.

[2] It will be noted that this corresponds precisely to the definition
as well as to the example of the anagogic sense which we find in
the *Convivio*.

[3] And also where this veil does not exist, that is, in the narration of
the antecedents of the action, what is told of Dante's soul has reference
anagogically to the human soul, guided likewise in the straight way
before the fall of Adam and Eve.

But the letter, the allegory, and the anagoge, which the poet-theologian must have had all together in his mind during the composition of the *Commedia* (of which they form the entire contents, both open and hidden), have a common aim, which is the same that we said true and lofty poetry should have, according to the mediæval conception. This is, to impart to the individual and to human society (*the ethical and political aim*) philosophic and spiritual teachings — *philosophica documenta* and *documenta spiritualia* or *revelata* [1] — in which lies the " doctrine " to be drawn from the poem. And in this way we find the last of the four senses, the *moral*, which every reader (as has been said) must go intently noting, if he is " to take fruit of his reading."

In Dante's masterpiece all these four senses appear woven together in one organic whole ; in which each one, while it fulfills its own office, works with the others to the attainment of that supreme end which the author proposed to himself in composing his poem.

[1] *De monarchia*, treatise iii, chap. 16.

CHAPTER III

THE "VEIL"[1]: PARABLE OR IMAGERY

I. SCENE OF THE IMAGINARY ACTION. 1. Scene of the prologue on earth. 2. Topography of the Dantesque otherworld and, particularly, of Hell. 3. Moral classification of Hell. 4–5. Material and moral classification of Purgatory and Paradise.

II. THE IMAGINARY ACTION. 1–2. Dante in the "great desert," in the "dark country," and in the "infernal valley." 3–4. Dante on the mountain of the Earthly Paradise and on the table-land which crowns it. 5. Dante through the nine heavens and in the Empyrean.

I. SCENE OF THE IMAGINARY ACTION

1. Scene of the prologue on earth. The imaginary action of the *Commedia*, that is, the visionary journey of Dante, has its scene laid first in the world of the living; afterwards (from the beginning of canto iii) in the bowels of the earth, in the lower uninhabited hemisphere,[2] and in the celestial spheres. Let us see how the poet represents the places through which he pictures himself as journeying.

In the world of the living, a *valley*,[3] a *slope*,[4] and a *mountain*[5] form the scene which he puts before us. The valley is clothed with a thick wood; but where it is situated is not told us, since these places in the prologue of the poem are the figures of abstract conceptions, which do not

---

[1] [There is a misprint in the original edition. This word should read "velo," not "vero."]

[2] [The hemisphere of water, through which he passes from Hell to Purgatory.]

[3] *Inf.* i, 14–15 (and cf. xv, 49–51).   [4] Ibid. 29.

[5] Ibid. 13, 21, 77–78.

correspond to any objective reality. And the word " valley "
should be here taken in the sense which Dante usually
gives it whenever he makes use of it merely as the means
of a poetic suggestion. *Valley* is, in such a case, not a bit
of land between mountains, but a *shell*, a " deep cavity in
the ground," like that one which, lying under the level of
the land which emerges, is filled by the waters of the sea.[1]
This cavity ends at the foot of a mountain, and here we
must imagine a *slope*, that is (to use the words of Giambullari and Gelli), a space lying below a more pronounced
ascent " somewhat elevated, but not much, since one can
mount quite easily almost without being aware of it." [2] To
show that this slope is not yet that " steep " which he
indicates a bit further on (verse 31), but a slight incline,
the poet adds that tortured verse " so that the firm foot
was always the lower " — an almost mathematical designation of the manner in which one proceeds on the aforesaid
slope. And this manner is, notwithstanding its inclination,
the same as walking on a plain.[3]

[1] Study the following passages : *Inf.* iv, 8 ; ix, 16–17 ; x, 134–136 (and
cf. xi, 4–5); xii, 40 and 86; xiv, 115 and 136. *Purg.* i, 45 ; xxiv, 84. *Parad.*
ix, 82–84; xvii, 138. And we may add that the ten broad ditches
where the " malign field of Malebolge " is hollowed out are valleys for
Dante, as is the cup in the steep of Purgatory " where the hillside
makes a lap of itself." In addition see my *Significati*, i, 75–77.

[2] See the *Commento sopra il I canto dell' Inf. di P. F. Giambullari*, in
the Appendix to the volume of M. Barbi, *Della fortuna di Dante nel
sec. xvi*, Pisa, Nistri, 1890, p. 377.

[3] Only when one is walking on a plain is
the firm foot (that is to say, that one of the two
which alternately bears the weight of the body)
the lower of the two. When one ascends it is
different. Let us suppose that a person starts
from a certain point x on a strongly inclined plane, having his feet on
the same level. He will move one to ascend and will carry it to y ; at
that moment the firm foot will be the lower of the two. Then, resting
his firm foot at y, he will raise at the same time the other (hitherto at x)

This slope extends from the edge of the wooded valley to "the beginning of the steep," forming a kind of foot-hill or scarp of the mountain (of indefinite length), not unlike that plain sloping to its lowest edge, which we shall see surrounding the mountain of the Earthly Paradise, conceived by Dante in the center of the lower hemisphere. And this real mountain, the antipodes of Jerusalem, which, girt about by a slightly inclined plain,[1] emerges from the cavity which is filled by the waters of the ocean, has an indisputable analogy with the imaginary mountain which is separated by a slope from the wooded shell where the action of the poem begins, and is without a determined situation. And this shell or "valley," in its turn, seems analogous to the "infernal valley." Also, through the latter there flows down an imaginary "stream,"[2] just as an actual river flows through that pit. Also down its "dark hillside" a fanciful path descends, just as a real "savage road"[3] descends the infernal steep. And this is the "deep and savage road"[4] which goes down to the

to move it to y, and thence to z, a higher point than y. In the first case the "firm foot" will be the higher during the whole step; in the second case it will be the higher during the first part of the step and the lower during the second part, and so on until the ascent is finished. Need we add that the same thing happens in the descent, only in an opposite direction?

[1] This plain which surrounds the mountain of the Earthly Paradise, Dante would not have hesitated to call a "slope," as does Petrarch in like case. Cf. *Il canzoniere di Francesco Petrarca*, ccx, 2 (ed. Modigliani, p. 42).

[2] This is a poetic figure, to be taken in the same sense as the valley, the slope, and the hill. The poet does not speak of it in the first canto, because he speaks there only of the dangers of which he was aware, and he had not noticed that he was on the bank of a stream more raging than the sea itself, which, rushing down into the valley from the edge of the slope, threatened to sweep him away. But Lucia had remarked it well, and we shall give the symbolic meaning of this in its proper place.   [3] *Inf.* viii, 91; ix, 100; xii, 92; xxi, 84.   [4] *Inf.* ii, 142.

gate of Hell — it is the life of damnation, the *falsest* path
contrary to the *truest*,[1] that is, opposed to the " right way," [2]
which we ought to imagine towards the right up the steep
of the " delectable mountain."

Here is, in profile, the topography of the prologue of
the *Commedia*.

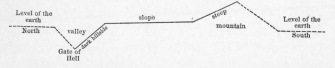

**2. The topography of the Dantesque otherworld and,
particularly, of Hell.** Having left behind the world of the
living, let us see now how the poet has thought out the
three kingdoms of the dead.

The universe, according to Dante, left the divine hands
fashioned after the following manner :

Around the Earth as a common center nine heavens
revolve, the more swiftly as they are the farther removed
from it ; and this is all contained in one motionless heaven
of pure light, the Empyrean. In this latter is the City of
God, the Heavenly Paradise, with its nine orders of the
three angelic hierarchies. In that part of the Earth which
looks toward this city, and in the direction of the latter, an
island emerges from the waters with which that hemisphere
veiled itself when Lucifer (the created being that stood
nearest God) fell headlong into it. And on this island
there arises a mountain, higher than any other in the
world, on the summit of which (that is, on the point of
the Earth nearest Heaven) the Earthly Paradise is situated
on a table-land covered with woods and flowers. Around
this mountain, and covering the whole surface of the

---

[1] See *Conv.* treatise iv, chap. 12.   [2] *Inf.* i, 3 and 12.

hemisphere of which it occupies the central point, lies the Ocean ; in the opposite hemisphere there is the " great dry land," [1] the " *arida*," [2] that is, the habitable earth. Finally, from the center of the terraqueous globe towards the surface of the hemisphere which is opposite God, there rises a conical cavity, which is indeed the seat of the angels who were turned from God, that is, of the demons. And at the point of this inverted cone (that is, in the center of the Earth) is fixed Lucifer himself, arising from the navel up, in the prison which shall be his kingdom for eternity.

Before the creation of man this cavity, that is, Hell, was (as it was later and ever will be) a rocky shell of a very considerable diameter at the part nearest the surface, and growing gradually smaller as it approaches the center of the Earth. But at that time only the lower part, much narrower, was inhabited. Here, girt with iron walls and with towers and moats, the city of Dis, that is, of Satan, enclosed Satan himself and the others " driven from heaven." At that time, except this city, there was nothing but a stony desert. Only, in the vestibule of the dark places, between the entrance (then closed) to the " valley of the abyss " and the edge of the valley itself in the " dark country " which this surrounds, there was a throng of those rejected by Justice as well as by Mercy — the pusillanimous angels " who were not rebels, nor were faithful to God, but were for themselves." [3]

Then man came upon the earth. He came, good and immortal, with his face turned towards his creator on the summit of that mountain " which rises highest towards heaven." But even up there, in that " lofty garden,"

---

[1] *Inf*. xxxiv, 113.   [2] Genesis i, 9–10.   [3] *Inf*. iii, 38–39.

there comes the malignant breath of the "wicked worm" shut up in the bowels of the earth. And so man (who has become a sinner) is expelled from the place "chosen for his nest," and consigned to the opposite hemisphere, *aversus a Deo*, like Lucifer and the demons. Like them he is condemned (before it pleased the Word of God to descend among us) to the "eternal prison,"[1] to the sub-terranean "dismal shell."[2] The latter, as the centuries pass, gradually becomes peopled with deploring souls and adapts itself to its new use. Within a mountain in the island of Crete there stands a statue in the form of a great Old Man, composed of several metals. From this statue tears drop, which, collected, pierce the rock and wind their way underground, where they form the infernal rivers Acheron, Styx, and Phlegethon, which finally form the lake of Cocytus. The ignoble souls are ferried over these rivers — where in their descent they form a marsh either around the whole shell (*the Acheron*) or around the last pit, i.e. the city of Dis (*the Styx*) — by two boat-men, Charon and Phlegyas. They are awaited by a judge, Minos, who examines each one for fault, to see what "place of hell" befits him. Over each place there pre-sides either a demon in the semblance of a beast (*Cer-berus, Pluto*) or a monster half-beast and half-man (*the Minotaur, Geryon*). Down in the "woeful city" Centaurs and Devils torture the souls of the sinners. And finally, around the "dismal hole" upon which the rocks of the valley of the abyss rest, tower the Giants, like Lucifer rebellious against the divine power. Thus the bank of Hell has come to enclose as in a sack all the evil of the world,[3] — not only that of which the Holy Scriptures speak,

[1] *Purg.* i, 41.   [2] *Inf.* ix, 16.   [3] Cf. *Inf.* vii, 18.

but also that of ancient mythology. So in the Dantesque conception we see the Christian ideas grafted upon the old stories and upon the topographical peculiarities of the Greek Hades and the Latin Avernus.

Such is the "infernal valley" according to Alighieri. But we should add immediately that this poetic conception corresponds to physical and mathematical laws only in its broad lines. People have tried to reconcile it in all its details, fixing rigorously the dimensions of the whole valley and of all its divisions. But in doing so we must force the poet's words to say what they do not say. Consequently it seems preferable to believe that he forgot these laws from time to time, or wished to forget them, and was content occasionally to quote figures and measures which would give credit to his fancies by lending them a certain appearance of mathematical precision. It will be sufficient, then, to remember the following facts : (1) that the walls of the great funnel (to which we may compare the infernal shell imagined by Dante), girt within by slightly inclined circular banks, descend from one to another almost vertically, so that the passage from one circle to the next (the "point where the descent is")[1] is of necessity formed by a sort of rough stairway or landslide ; these walls contract as we descend towards the point of the cone, so that they finally form a cavity which may be called a "hole" in comparison with the "broad jaws" of the pit ; (2) that the edge of this great shell is surrounded by a sloping space (the dark "country" mentioned above), within which the river Acheron rims the shell itself ; (3) that, of the NINE circles into which this shell seems divided, the first forms Limbo, and the fifth

[1] *Inf.* vi, 114

(which is in its whole circumference full of the mud of the Styx, except a strip between the bank and the "fen"), while on the same level with the sixth, is separated from it by the walls of the city of Dis; this sixth circle forms around the last pit a sloping space (a "country" similar to that which surrounds the whole valley); (4) that the seventh circle consists of (*a*) "a broad ditch bent in an arc," brimming over with the boiling red waters of Phlegethon ("the river of the blood"), (*b*) a wood, also turning in a circle, and contained within the ditch, (*c*) a plain, likewise circular, all covered with a dense sand (the "great sand") and contained within the wood; (5) that the eighth circle is a round "field" declining from every direction to the center, and furrowed by ten "moats," or "valleys," or "pouches," whence the name of *Malebolge* (Evil Pouches); among these are elevations of land, or "embankments," joined by bridges, as in the accompanying profile drawing of these pouches;

(6) that in the center of the field of Malebolge "yawns

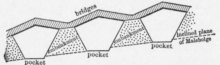

a pit," by which is the descent to the bottom of the valley of the abyss,—which is the bottom "for all the Universe," [1] — where a frozen lake (*Cocytus*) forms the ninth and last circle, which is divided into four concentric zones, Caina, Antenora, Ptolomea, and Judecca; (7) that in the central hole of this "ice" Lucifer, *rex Inferni*, is fixed (the

---

[1] The famous verses " For to describe the bottom of the whole Universe is no enterprise to take up in jest" (*Inf.* xxxii, 7–8) should be translated thus : " It is no slight undertaking to describe the bottom of the whole Universe." [The difficulty here indicated as existing in the original Italian has been removed in the English translation : Ché non è impresa da pigliare a gabbo *Descriver fondo a tutto l'Universo.*]

middle point of whose body coincides with the center of the earth — the point "to which from every part all weighty things are drawn "). This figure is represented as an enormous and monstrous " structure," like a windmill, with three faces of different colors and six great bat wings which he flaps continually.[1]

The whole infernal cavity may be then represented much as in the following figure.

Structure of Hell

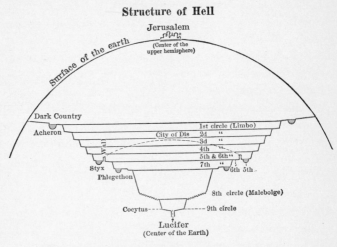

3. Moral classification of Hell. The seat of the " truly dead," in the poet's imagination, includes the " valley of the abyss " and the " country " which surrounds it. In this " country," in the space which stretches from the gate of the immense cavern to the " great river " (*the Acheron*), over which must pass all " those who die in the wrath of God," are punished the abject or " pusillanimous," held in

[1] Lucifer has six wings, in large part because he is a seraphim, and seraphim " make a cowl for themselves with their six wings " (*Parad.* ix, 78).

disdain by God's justice and mercy. Among these are prominent those who, while more highly favored by Heaven, committed a greater sin in not putting these gifts to profit. The valley of the abyss "insacks" in its nine circles all "the evils of the universe," that is, all those guilty of the sins which proceed from moral evil (*malitia*), from an "evil disposition" or moral infirmity. This perverse "disposition," according to Aristotle's "Ethics," which, as we have seen,[1] Dante adopts, is threefold : the dispositions which "Heaven does not wish" are *incontinence, moral evil*, and *bestiality*.[2] Incontinence offends God less, and incurs less blame,[3] because it is "moral evil arising from passion" (*ex passione*), as St. Thomas teaches in his commentary on the "Ethics" of the philosopher. And since simple *moral evil* and *bestiality* (which is bestial moral evil) have injury (*injustificatio*, ἀδίκημα) for an end, they incur "hatred" in Heaven [4] because they constitute "moral evil from choice" (*ex electione*), *fixed moral evil* (*certa malitia*).

Wherefore the upper part of Hell, outside the city of Dis, is occupied by the incontinent ; the lower part, that is, the last pit inclosed by the glowing walls, is the abode of the "felons," who were guilty of "moral evil from choice." Those of the incontinent who could not restrain their concupiscent sensuous appetite are in the part before

[1] See above, p. 18.

[2] Vergil says to Dante in canto xi (where he explains the moral classification of the valley of the abyss) : "Dost thou not remember those words with which THY *Ethics* treats in full of the three dispositions that Heaven abides not, incontinence, wickedness, and mad bestiality?" (ll. 79–83).

[3] "And how incontinence less offends God, and incurs less blame" (*Inf.* xi, 83–84).

[4] "Of every wickedness that acquires hate in heaven injury is the end" (*Inf.* xi, 22–23).

the Styx in three divisions : Circle II (the *carnal sinners*), Circle III (the *gluttons*), Circle IV (the *evil spenders*). Those of the incontinent who could not restrain their irascible sensuous appetite (that is, the *wrathful*) are in the Styx, which surrounds the walls of the "ruddy city," and is Circle V. These are divided into three troops,[1] according as they yielded to fury,[2] rancor,[3] or inflation (tumefaction) of mind ("arrogance").[4]   In their turn the "felons" who populate the city of the Demon are in three divisions, placed in the last three narrower circles of the valley ("lesser circles"). The first of these circles (VII of the entire hell) is the abode of those who have sinned through *bestial moral evil*, or *bestiality;* that is, the *violent*, for that "moral evil from choice," which acts after the fashion of beasts, uses force as the means of doing injury.[5] And the violent are divided into three rounds, according as they did violence to the neighbor, to themselves, or to God.[6] The

---

[1] See what is said of this division in my *Significati*, part i, chap. 1, §§ 13–14.

[2] These are the wrathful that Aristotle calls *acuti*. Partially immersed in the swamp of the Styx, they strike and bite each other.

[3] These are the wrathful that Aristotle calls *amari*. Completely immersed in the Styx, they "are sullen" in the black mire, just as they were "sullen" in the world, "bearing within [the] sluggish fume," — that is to say, brooding over their wrath so as not to be able to apply themselves to works which would merit eternal life.

[4] These are the wrathful that Aristotle calls χαῦνοι, "presumptuous." Mingled with the other "furious," they pay dear for the acts of anger committed because the world did not do them the honor which they arrogated to themselves, since they considered themselves "great kings." Among them was Filippo Argenti, an "arrogant person" (*Inf.* viii, 46).   [5] Cf. *Inf.* xi, 23–24 and 28.

[6] Against the neighbor one can do violence to his body and to his property; against one's self, likewise to the body and to the property; against God, to the body, or to nature (the daughter of God), or to nature and to art (the daughter of nature, and hence, "as it were, grandchild to God"). From this arise further distinctions in the three varieties of the violent.

second and third of these same circles (VIII and IX of the entire hell) are the abode of those who have sinned through true *moral evil;* that is, the *fraudulent.* For this "moral evil from choice," which acts after the fashion of man, uses fraud (the "evil proper to man") as the means of doing injury. And one of these circles contains the fraudulent in whom no trust is put, distributed in the ten valleys or moats of Malebolge : in the first, *seducers* (for the benefit of others or for themselves) ; in the second, *flatterers;* in the third, *simonists;* in the fourth, *diviners;* in the fifth, *barrators;* in the sixth, *hypocrites;* in the seventh, *robbers;* in the eighth, *fraudulent counselors;* in the ninth, *sowers of discord;* in the tenth, *falsifiers.* The other circle, that is, the last of the entire valley, the bottom of the infernal pit, is the abode of the fraudulent in whom trust is put, that is, the traitors, distributed in the four concentric zones that surround Lucifer : in the first, *traitors to kindred* (Caina) ; in the second, *traitors to country* (Antenora) ; in the third, *traitors to friends* (Ptolomea) ; in the fourth, *traitors to benefactors* (Judecca).

In this distribution of sinners in the infernal valley according to the threefold Aristotelian division of *moral evil* or "evil disposition" of man, Circles I and VI are excluded. Dante has reserved them for a kind of moral weakness that Aristotle, who lived "before Christianity," could not know : infidelity. And he has placed that infidelity which proceeds from "lack of faith" in the first circle of the entire abyss (as a negative sin[1] less grave than the others) ; and that which proceeds from "opposition to faith" (*infidelitas secundum contrarietatem ad fidem*),

[1] Those guilty of infidelity, "*secundum puram negationem*," are punished "not for doing, but for not doing," that is, "for not having faith" (*Purg.* vii, 25 and 28).

which is called heresy (*haeresis*) inasmuch as it "implies choice," in the sixth circle, which is the first of those comprised within the city of Dis, the abode of "moral evil from choice."

We should add, moreover, that Dante, always scrupulously orthodox, does not impugn the ecclesiastical division by adopting the above Aristotelian scheme. As the other five mortal sins are punished in the circles of the incontinent,[1] so pride, the mother and root of every sin, and envy, almost inseparable from it, should be promiscuously punished in the city of the felons, the true *unjust*. "Every wickedness that acquires hate in heaven," whether bestial or fraudulent, is the fault of one of these. And that is why we find at the bottom of hell the proud Giants of mythology and him who "with accursed pride" occasioned the fall of a part of the angels.[2]

In conclusion, the arrangement of sinners that Dante, following the "Nicomachean Ethics" and St. Thomas's commentary on them, has thought out for his Hell may be represented as in the appended table.

4. Material and moral classification of Purgatory. From the bottom of the valley of the abyss we approach the lower hemisphere by a "hidden road"[3] which comes out in the island at the antipodes of Jerusalem, where the mountain of the Earthly Paradise[4] rises from the "wide

---

[1] Among them *sloth* as well, closely connected either with cowardice of mind or pusillanimity, or with rancor or repressed anger ("sluggish fume").   [2] Cf. *Parad.* xxix, 55–57.

[3] This road ascends in the cavity made by Lucifer in his fall from heaven, when he pierced the earth on this side (as far as the center, where he remained fixed). Cf. *Inf.* xxxiv, 111 ff.

[4] It is more exact to call it by this name, rather than the mountain of Purgatory, since the latter is only temporary (from the Redemption to the Last Judgment).

MORAL EVIL (or evil disposition)

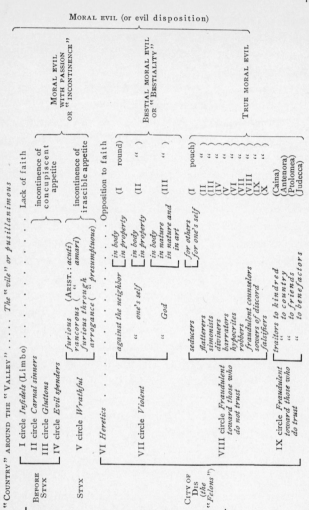

MORAL EVIL WITH PASSION OR "INCONTINENCE"

BESTIAL MORAL EVIL OR "BESTIALITY"

TRUE MORAL EVIL

"COUNTRY" AROUND THE "VALLEY" . . . . . The "vile" or pusillanimous

Lack of faith

incontinence of concupiscent appetite

incontinence of irascible appetite

Opposition to faith

in body / in property (I round)
in body / in property (II ")
in body / in nature and in art (III ")

for others (I pouch)
for one's self (II ")
(III)
(IV)
(V)
(VI)
(VII)
(VIII)
(IX)
(X)

(Caina)
(Antenora)
(Ptolomea)
(Judecca)

furious (ARIST.: acuti)
rancorous (" : amari)
furious through arrogance (" : presumptuous)

against the neighbor
" one's self
" God

seducers
flatterers
simonists
diviners
barrators
hypocrites
robbers
Fraudulent counselors
sowers of discord
falsifiers

traitors to kindred
" to country
" to friends
" to benefactors

BEFORE STYX

I circle Infidels (Limbo)
II circle Carnal sinners
III circle Gluttons
IV circle Evil spenders

STYX

V circle Wrathful

VI circle Heretics

VII circle Violent

CITY OF DIS (the "Felons")

VIII circle Fraudulent toward those who do not trust

IX circle Fraudulent toward those who do trust

"VALLEY OF THE ABYSS"

waves." In the "country" around this mountain those who *died in contumacy of the Church*, and who owe their salvation to the fact that they turned to God at the last, expiate temporarily their sin. Like the "pusillanimous," who are eternally punished in the "country" around the valley, these too have not done actual good. This was not because they did not want to, but rather because they had not the opportunity, since they died immediately after their conversion.

The mountain has a very abrupt and very long steep,[1] where the *negligent*, who have repented only at their last moment, either through laziness or a violent death, await the moment of their expiation. Among these, in a flowery valley (which is a dip in the rise of the mountain), are kings, princes, and lords, who neglected the duties inherent in their office. At the highest point of this steep is the entrance to Purgatory, through a gate which seems a cleft in a wall. This gate, narrow and closed, at the top of the steep of a mountain, which one gains with much fatigue through a strait "passage," is to be contrasted with that of Hell, wide and open, at the bottom of the incline of a valley, to which one descends so easily by the "deep and savage road." This is the gate of the kingdom of heaven,

[1] Even when he is on this steep Dante does not see its end, and, after having traversed a considerable part of it has need of supernatural aid (*Lucia*), which raises him, while asleep, near to that cliff which encircles Purgatory. Above this point the clouds do not rise, because that part of the mountain which is subject to atmospheric changes ends with the steep (cf. *Purg.* xxi, 43–54). If we add to this steep the seven degrees of Purgatory itself, and the table-land which crowns it, that is, the Earthly Paradise, we can imagine ourselves very near the first heaven, the heaven of the Moon. Dante seems to have followed the opinions of those (among whom is Peter Lombard) who conceive the Earthly Paradise as "secretum et in alto situm, usque ad lunarem circulum pertingentem."

St. Peter's gate, guarded by his "vicar," [1] an angel, and which leads to life as the other leads to perdition.[2] But one does not ascend through it to heaven without having first mounted the "stairway" of the seven steps,[3] which the Supreme Artificer cut in the precipitous walls of the upper part of the mountain, when it pleased him to make again accessible to "human spirits" its peak, whence one ascends to Him.[4] Jesus, by suffering martyrdom on the summit of Golgotha near Jerusalem, opened once more to mortals, by giving its keys to the first of his Apostles, the gate through which one mounts to the Celestial Jerusalem, after having attained the antipodal summit.[5] From that time those who are destined for this Celestial Jerusalem start from the mouth of the Tiber under protection of the church, cross the Ocean over which an angel brings them, land at the island, mount the steep of the mountain, and then go through the *janua Cœli*, up over

---

[1] Cf. *Inf.* i, 134, and *Purg.* xxi, 54.

[2] "For wide is the gate, and broad is the way, that leadeth to destruction. . . . Strait is the gate, and narrow is the way, which leadeth unto life" (Matthew vii, 13–14).

[3] Cf. *Purg.* xxi, 20–21, and xxvi, 145–146 (in the last of these lines the true reading is "this stairway").

[4] It is clear that this stairway, that is, Purgatory, did not exist, or was not used, before the Redemption of Christ, — when "human spirits were not saved," when all, after death, descended to the Acheron in order to go to Limbo if innocent, or to Hell if evil. At that time, also, the earth was almost joined to heaven by means of the very lofty mountain on whose summit man enjoyed the felicity of this world (near to God, and turned towards him). But an angel with a flaming sword forbade its access to mortals who, after the first sin, were relegated to the opposite hemisphere, *averse to God*. Now an angel still guards the way to that peak ("the way of the tree of life," Genesis iii, 24). But he represents pity instead of vengeance, since he is clothed with the habit of the penitents and uses his flaming sword only to imprint on the foreheads of the repentant the wounds which they are to wash away before attaining the summit.

[5] [The Earthly Paradise, antipodal to Golgotha.]

the stairway which is beyond that steep, over the table-land of the Earthly Paradise on the summit of the mountain, and thus come and occupy the seat which awaits them in the City of God.

But it is given to very few of these souls to make the entire journey soon after death. The greater number stop for a time along the way, especially on the circular steps of the aforesaid "stairway," that is to say, in Purgatory. This is formed by seven "landings" (*ledges* or *circuits* or *rounds* or *cornices*) by which the mountain, progressively contracting in the part above the long "steep," is circled at various heights. Here, by means of the "torments," those "who have made good ends and spirits already elect" cleanse themselves from the *guilt which merits temporary punishment* proceeding from the *disorderly direction* (which has alone remained in them) *of the "appetite of their minds" in respect to good;* since their admission, through grace, to the state of penitence has taken away the *guilt which merits eternal punishment* (proceeding from the *aversion to God* in which mortal sin, in its essence, consists), as well as the blemish produced by the deformity of sin. Such disorderly direction generates a disorderly state in the "inclination of the mind," that is, in *love*,[1] on account of which the mind "inclines" either towards the true good "with less zeal than it ought," or towards the corruptible good "with more zeal than it ought." In the first case the disorderly state of love consists in a defect ("little vigor") and is called *sloth;* in the second it consists in an excess ("too much vigor"), and is called *avarice, gluttony, luxury,* according as the

[1] See the definition of love which Vergil gives in *Purg.* xviii, 19 ff.

object to which the appetite of the mind is inclined is money, food, or women. But the corruptible good to which the mind inclines may likewise be an evil under the appearance of good (*malum sub ratione boni*). In such a case the disorderly state of love consists merely in bending the mind towards it ("evil object"), and is called *pride*, *envy*, *wrath*, according as it is the love of one's own excellence, or sullenness at another's success, or appetite for vengeance.

This is the gravest disorderly state; the most excusable is that which proceeds from excess. Wherefore the *capital vices* or "disorderly states of love" follow each other in decreasing enormity through the rounds of Purgatory in this order : *pride*, *envy*, *wrath*, *sloth*, *avarice*, *gluttony*, *luxury*.

So the "second realm" of the dead, where "the human spirit is purified, and becomes worthy to ascend to heaven," is, like the first, threefold; and, like it, divided into nine parts, plus one, which brings this nine, the multiple of three, to ten, the perfect number.[1] As the realm of damnation consists of the gloomy "country" and the "valley" divided into nine circles, so the realm of purification consists of the "country" around the mountain and of the mountain itself, likewise divided into nine parts; that is, the steep where "one waits," the seven rounds of Purgatory where the soul is purified from disorderly inclination, and the Earthly Paradise. The latter is formed of a delightful forest, among whose trees towers the "despoiled plant" of the *knowledge of good and evil*,[2] and where, in the waters of the rivers Lethe and Eunoe, of supernatural

---

[1] Cf. *Vita nova*, chap. 29 [Norton, 30]; *Conv.* treatise ii, chap. 15.
[2] [The Tree of the Knowledge of Good and Evil.]

origin, — the first having the virtue of removing the memory of sin, the second of restoring the memory of every good deed, — is revived that natural inclination which leads us to God.

Structure and classification of the Second Realm

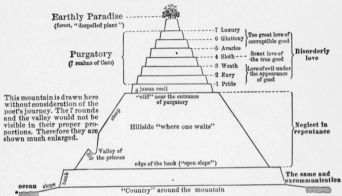

5. **Classification of Paradise.** And the realm of beatitude, as conceived by Dante symmetrical with the other two, also shows an analogous division. The nine concentric heavens of the Ptolemaic system, revolving around the earth, may be divided into three parts, corresponding to the persons of the Trinity, since they bear the same relation to the nine orders of angels as there is between " the example and the exemplar." [1] And these orders are divided into three hierarchies, according as they have to do with the power of the Father, the wisdom of the Son, or the love of the Holy Ghost.[2] So to the first "triad" of the angelic orders (*Seraphim, Cherubim, Thrones*) correspond the " Prime Mover " [3] (which

---

[1] *Parad.* xxviii, 55–56.   [2] Cf. *Conv.* treatise ii, chap. 6.

[3] Better translated, "First moving heaven" or "first heaven to

moves the other heavens while inclosing them in itself), the Starry (or "heaven of the fixed stars"), and the heaven of the planet Saturn. To the second triad (*Dominations, Virtues, Powers*) correspond the heavens of the planets Jupiter, Mars, and the Sun; and to the third triad (*Principalities, Archangels, Angels*), the heavens of the planets Venus, Mercury, and the Moon. The Empyrean closes and, as it were, seals this realm of eternal peace, reducing (as usual) the multiple of three to unity.

And all the blessed have their seat with God and the angels in the Empyrean heaven, which "is not in space and has no poles."[1] They show themselves to Dante in the various heavens only because God wishes to give him a sensible proof that the attainment, while alive, of loving rather than doing, of contemplating rather than struggling, etc., procures one a more or less lofty seat in the *civitas Dei*, according as the heaven whose *virtue* ("influence") disposes to one or the other of such things is more or less near the Empyrean, the common abode.[2] The "city" of the blessed[3] has the form of a vast amphitheater of more than a thousand rows, divided into two semicircles by opposite vertical lines, made respectively by the seats of the Virgin and other Hebrew women, and by those of the Baptist and other continuers of

move," thus rendering the Latin "primum mobile." The fact that it does move the other heavens is secondary, and is not provided for in its name. The true "Prime Mover" is God.   [1] *Parad.* xxii, 67.

[2] Thus, for example, Folco of Marseilles is in the third order of the blessed, because he was "imprinted" by the power of the third heaven, that of Venus, which disposes to love. The souls which compose the *eagle* ("the ensign of the world and of its leaders") are in the sixth order of the elect, because the justice which they practiced is the "effect" of the sixth heaven, that of Jupiter (cf. *Parad.* ix, 95–96, and xviii, 115–117).   [3] Cf. *Parad.* xxx, 130.

his work. One of these semicircles is occupied by those who believed in Christ to come, the other by "those who turned their faces on Christ already come."[1] In this amphitheater, from the middle up, the spirits are placed in different rows according to their merit.[2] Among them the *defective* (who appeared to Dante in the *Moon*), because they did not keep their vows, sit in the lowest and most contracted part.[3] Then come successively, as the celestial amphitheater "spreads wide," those spirits who were *active* through desire for honor and glory (who appeared to Dante in *Mercury*), the *loving spirits*, the *wise spirits*, the *spirits militant* for love of the faith, the *just spirits*, and the *contemplative spirits* (who appeared to Dante respectively in *Venus*, in the *Sun*, in *Mars*, in *Jupiter*, and in *Saturn*). Indeterminate is the number of the "more than thousand seats" in this amphitheater which are assigned to each of these "orders" of spirits. And since all the blessed have the same aspect, Dante could not have distinguished one of these orders from the other, without the providential vision of each order in its corresponding planet, which was granted him by God. And before it was given him to contemplate the "lofty seat" of the blessed in the Empyrean, he has previously had the vision of the entire throng of the elect, inasmuch as they participated in the triumph of Christ (in the *Heaven of the Stars*) ; and, finally, that of the nine orders of the three angelic hierarchies as they are moved by God, and correspond to the nine heavens (in the *Prime Mover*).

---

[1] *Parad.* xxxii, 27.

[2] From the middle down, on the other hand, "they are seated for no merit of their own." Here are the *babes*, dead "ere they had true power of choice" (*Parad.* xxxii, 40 ff.).

[3] The celestial sphere "which is least exalted" (*Parad.* iv, 38–39).

Classification of Paradise

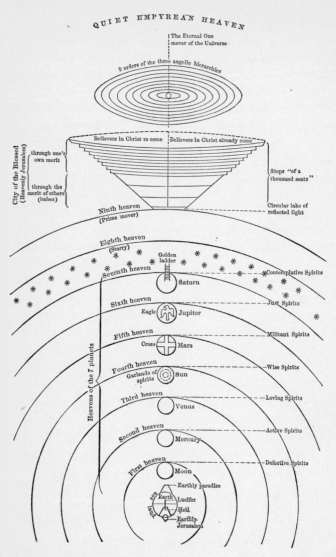

QUIET EMPYREAN HEAVEN

The Eternal One
mover of the Universe

9 orders of the three angelic hierarchies

Believers in Christ to come | Believers in Christ already come

City of the Blessed
(Heavenly Jerusalem)

through one's own merit

through the merit of others (babes)

Steps "of a thousand seats"

Ninth heaven (Prime mover)

Circular lake of reflected light

Eighth heaven (Starry)

Seventh heaven — Golden ladder — Saturn — Contemplative Spirits

Sixth heaven — Eagle — Jupiter — Just Spirits

Fifth heaven — Cross — Mars — Militant Spirits

Fourth heaven — Garlands of spirits — Sun — Wise Spirits

Third heaven — Venus — Loving Spirits

Second heaven — Mercury — Active Spirits

First heaven — Moon — Defective Spirits

Heavens of the 7 planets

Earthly paradise
Earth — Lucifer
Hell
Earthly Jerusalem

53

II. The Imaginary Action

**1. Dante in the " great desert," in the " dark country,"
and in the upper division of the " infernal valley."** Having
reviewed the scene in which the imaginary action of the
Comedy takes place, let us briefly examine this action.

At the age of thirty-five Dante becomes aware that he
is in a dark wood. He comes out of it, and when he has
reached the edge of the valley in which it lies, he advances
towards the steep of a beautiful mountain. An " ounce "
(panther or leopard) bars his way. Nevertheless he hopes
to overcome this obstacle; but two other wild beasts oppose
him successively, a lion and a wolf, and the latter drives
him back towards the brink of the valley. He is on the
point of plunging down, when Vergil, who has ascended
the " dark hillside " of the wooded valley from the infernal
valley underneath, offers to save him from the savage valley.
This is to be accomplished by the only way which remains,
that is to say, by the road which goes to Hell, passes
through it, ascends to the lower hemisphere, and continues on up the mount of purgation. Dante accepts ; but
he is immediately assailed by cowardice, so that Vergil is
constrained to explain to him that he is sent to the aid of
her friend by Beatrice, at the instigation of the Madonna
(and through the mediation of a saint, Lucia). Then the
poet advances along the wooded valley behind his " leader,"
and reaches the gate of Hell.

After having crossed the dark country (which lies under
the surface of the earth) where the pusillanimous are constrained to follow a flag and are pricked on by wasps and
gadflies, and where he recognizes among the others him
" who made, through cowardice, the great refusal " (that

is, probably, Pope Celestine V); while he is in a sleeping state, caused by the light that is flashed at him by a wind which proceeds from the quaking earth, he is transported to the other side of the Acheron, the "evil river," over which the demon Charon ferries the souls lately arrived there from the world. On awakening, Dante finds himself on the edge of the valley of the abyss and descends into the first circle, Limbo. Here, where the spirits are in "woe" but not "torment," Homer, Horace, Ovid, and Lucan come to meet Vergil; then all together they enter a castle which receives the *great spirits* of antiquity upon a fair meadow. In the next circle (where the jurisdiction of Minos, the judge of Hell, begins) the poet finds the *carnal sinners*, borne on a whirlwind; and he speaks with that adulterous brother and sister-in-law, Paolo Malatesta and Francesca da Polenta.[1]

While he lies deprived of his senses by the pity with which these latter have inspired him, he is transported, without knowing how, to the third circle of the valley. This is occupied by the *gluttonous*, who languish in the rain, watched over by Cerberus, who has the aspect of a tripled-jawed dog. Here he speaks with the Florentine Ciacco. Thence he passes into the fourth circle, of which Plutus is the guardian, and which contains the *evil spenders* (misers and prodigals), moving against each other in two throngs from opposite directions, and pushing heavy weights with their breasts. Then they go through the fifth circle, where the *wrathful*, in the marsh of the Styx, either strike each other above the slime or are sullen under the mire. Here he and Vergil, after having made

---

[1] [Oftener called Francesca da Rimini, from the town over which the Polentas were lords.]

a long detour between the bank and the marsh, come to the foot of a tower on whose top two flames are burning, to which another has answered afar off. In response to these signals they see, hurrying in his little vessel, Phlegyas, whose duty it is to ferry over the Styx those who are destined for the city of Dis. The two poets enter this bark, thrust back into the mud a presumptuous and arrogant person, Filippo Argenti, cross the moat of the city, which has glowing towers and iron walls, and land at its entrance, which is guarded by a large number of devils. Vergil tries in vain to obtain entrance from them, and the two poets are forced to wait. During this delay, from the top of the loftiest tower the three Furies (Megæra, Alecto, and Tisiphone) threaten to turn Dante to stone by calling up Medusa; but Vergil prevents his looking upon the Gorgon, and soon after a heavenly messenger arrives, having crossed the Styx with dry feet. He opens the gate of the "ruddy city" and returns by the same way, without speaking.

2. Dante's journey through the city of Dis. Having thus entered the disputed fortress "without any strife," the two poets find themselves among the arch-heretics and their followers. These are within burning tombs, with their covers raised, with which the whole "spacious country" is dotted. From one of these sarcophagi issues the voice of Farinata degli Uberti, who appears soon after "from the girdle upwards." Dante converses with him and with Cavalcante dei Cavalcanti — father of Guido, the famous poet. Thence he and Vergil proceed towards the middle, that is, towards the deep abyss of the "nether Hell." While they are waiting behind the cover of a tomb in order that they may accustom their senses to the dismal blast exhaled from the pit, the Master explains to the poet what manner of spirits occupy the last "lesser circles." Then they descend into the seventh ledge, which is guarded by the Minotaur, half beast and half man. There Nessus, one of the centaurs who are continually patrolling the Phlegethon, carries Dante to the other shore, while pointing out the most notable among the spirits of the *violent against the neighbor*, who are immersed in that river of blood.

So the poets arrive in the wood which forms the second round of this circle. Here Pietro della Vigna, turned into a shrub like the other suicides, *violent against their own person*, explains the manner in which the soul is bound "in the hard knots," and the torture which is inflicted upon it by the Harpies, who make their nest in its branches; and Jacopo da S. Andrea, destroyer of his own property, is torn by black bitches. In the third round of the same circle, that is, on the sand upon which flames rain down, Vergil reproves the foolish boasting of one of the *violent against the divine*, Capaneus, and gives his disciple some account of the infernal rivers. Recognized by Brunetto Latini, another of these violent, Dante talks affectionately with him; and he also shows affection and pity for the three Florentines, Guido Guerra, Tegghiaio Aldobrandi, and Jacopo Rusticucci.

Into the pit, where is the descent to the next to the last circle, Vergil throws a cord with which Dante was girt; and at that signal we see Geryon come up, a serpent with a human face. The Master speaks with this beast while his scholar visits those *guilty of usury*, who are on the "extreme head" of that circle. Afterwards, following his guide on the crupper of the monster, Dante descends into

Malebolge. Here he visits in succession the *seducers* for the purposes of others or for themselves (scourged by demons), among whom are Venedico Caccianimico and Jason ; the *flatterers* (plunged into filth), among whom are Alessio Interminelli and Thais, celebrated by Terence ; the *simonists* (fixed in holes with the head down, their legs outside, and flames on the soles of their feet), among whom is Pope Nicholas III ; the *diviners* (with the head turned backwards), among whom are Amphiaraus, Tiresias, Manto, Guido Bonatti; the *barrators* (immersed in boiling pitch and hooked by devils), among whom are Ciampolo of Navarre, Fra Gomita, and Michael Zanche. In this pouch the poets are threatened and deceived by the demons, to whom Providence has assigned the government of the place, and by their leader Malacoda ; so that they hardly succeed in escaping, sliding down into the midst of the *hypocrites* (weighed down by cloaks of gilded lead), among whom are two Jovial Friars of Bologna (Catalano dei Malavolti and Loderingo degli Andalò) and Caiaphas, Anna, and the others of the Jewish Sanhedrim. Then they are obliged to climb the bank with the utmost fatigue, since the bridge is broken down at that point ; after which exertion, Dante, continuing his instructive visit, sees in the respective pouches the *robbers* (fated to be turned to ashes by the bite of a serpent, or to change into a serpent themselves), among whom are Vanni Fucci and the centaur Cacus ; the *fraudulent counselors* (each wrapped in a flame), among whom are Ulysses and Diomed, in a two-forked flame, and Guido da Montefeltro ; the *sowers of discord* (cut in pieces by the swords of demons), among whom are Mahomet, Pier da Medicina, Curio the Roman, Mosca de' Lamberti, Bertran de Born,

Geri del Bello ; and, finally, the *falsifiers* of various kinds : those *of metals* (covered with leprosy), *of persons* (biting themselves with rage as they run), *of money* (dropsical and athirst), *of words* (consumed by fever), among whom are Griffolino d'Arezzo, Capocchio, Gianni Schicchi, Myrrha, Master Adam, Sinon.

Having thus arrived at the center of the field of Malebolge, Dante sees towering up in a deep well (visible from the navel up) the Giants, — Nimrod, Ephialtes, Briareus, Antæus, etc. The latter, after being begged and flattered by Vergil, takes the two poets in his hand and places them at the bottom of the well. Here, in the ice of Cocytus, are the *traitors* (divided into four rounds, as we know), and the nearer we approach to the center, the more deeply are they submerged. Among them are Camicion dei Pazzi, Bocca degli Abati, Buoso da Duera, Count Ugolino della Gherardesca, Brother Alberigo. And finally, heralded by a wind that causes Dante to seek shelter behind Vergil, we see the frightful emperor of the abyss, intent on torturing with his three mouths Judas, Brutus, and Cassius. Gripping the "shaggy flanks," the two poets descend to the middle of this monster's body. Here (since it is the center of the earth) they turn their heads where their feet were, and wrenching themselves away from Lucifer, they mount by a secret way to the surface of the earth in the opposite hemisphere to ours, at the antipodes of Jerusalem.

3. Dante ascends the mountain of the Earthly Paradise. Now there shine before the marveling eyes of Dante the four stars which only our first parents, when in the garden of Eden, were permitted to admire. With their rays they illumine the venerable countenance of an old but still vigorous man, Cato. The latter, upon being

requested in a respectful manner, counsels Vergil to wash
the poet's face, to gird his loins with one of the reeds
which line the shore of that island where they now are,
and to take as a guide the sun, which is just rising. Vergil
obeys, and Dante, after having witnessed the disembark-
ing of a throng of souls guided by an angel, talks familiarly
with one of them, the soul of the musician Casella. Here
he starts to find the place where he may ascend, according
to the information given Vergil by a throng of spirits who
have their sojourn on the slope around the mountain
(*those dead in contumacy of the church*). Among these
is Manfred.

At that point the ascent of the mountain begins. It is
very wearisome, and the steep stretches farther than the
eye can carry. Upon this, the souls of the *negligent* await
their admission to Purgatory (which is as yet invisible,
higher up). Among these souls are Belacqua, Jacopo del
Cassero, Bonconte da Montefeltro, Pia dei Tolomei, Sordello. The latter leads the two poets to visit the spirits of
the princes and rulers, set apart in a flowering valley hollowed in the mountain side ; for "to go up by night is
not possible." Dante speaks with two of them (Nino
Visconti and Corrado Malaspina), while about them unrolls
a scene which is fertile in admonitions, — the arrival of a
tempter in the form of a serpent, which is suddenly put
to flight by two angels, come "from the bosom of Mary."

Afterwards Dante, raised by Lucia to the entrance of
Purgatory during his long sleep, finds himself near three
steps (one of white marble, another of dark "stone," the
third of vermilion porphyry) over which is the ascent to a
gate guarded by an angel. The latter marks seven P's on
Dante's forehead with the point of a sword, turns two

keys (one of gold and the other of silver), one after the other, in the lock of this gate, and throws it open. After crossing the threshold the poets mount to the first circular landing of Purgatory; they observe the examples of humility cut in the rock of the bank, speak with Omberto Aldo- brandesco and Oderisi da Gubbio (two of the *proud* ad- vancing, bent under heavy blocks of rock), and pass in review the examples of punished pride which are cut in the pavement. An angel obliterates with his wings one of the P's on Dante's brow, and directs the poets to the stairway which brings them to the next circle. Here, while voices rush through the air exhorting to charity or recall- ing examples of punished envy, the *envious* expiate their sin (their eyelids sewed together with iron wire). Among these are Sapia, Guido del Duca, and Rinieri da Calboli.

The ascent to the following ledges is always made in the same way, and, as always, there is an angel that erases one of the P's on the poet's forehead. On the third of these ledges Dante has ecstatic visions of examples of forbearance. Then he enters a thick and bitter smoke where the *wrathful* (among whom is Marco Lombardo) purge away their sin, and after coming out of this smoke he has visions of punished wrath. On the fourth ledge he sees the *slothful* running, in tears and singing, and crying aloud examples of zeal and of punished sloth. Among these souls is the abbot of St. Zeno. After these have dis- appeared he falls asleep, and dreams of the "ancient sorceress," whose effects are mourned in the three rounds which remain to be visited. Then in the first of these, where by day examples of the virtues opposed to avarice are cried out, and by night examples of punished avarice, he visits the *misers* and *prodigals* (lying face downwards with hands and feet bound). Among these are Pope Hadrian V and Hugh Capet, and Dante accompanies one of the prodigals, Statius, who, precisely at that moment after five hundred years and more, feels "a free volition for a better seat." Together the two poets ascend, conversing with him, to the ledge where the *gluttonous*, horribly wasted away, listen to voices recalling examples of temperance and of punished gluttony. Here Dante talks with Forese Donati and Bonagiunta da Lucca. Thence they mount to the seventh and last ledge, where the *luxurious*,[1] standing in the fire, cry out examples of chastity and of punished unchastity. Here Dante, after having conversed with Guido Guinizelli and Arnaut Daniel, is obliged, to his own great terror, to cross the flame which purifies the flesh, with his two companions. After this he can ascend to the summit of the mountain, but not without first having reposed and slept, dreaming of Leah, Rachel's sister, intent on picking flowers in a plain.

4. Dante's journey through the Earthly Paradise. Thus having reached the plain on the top of the mountain, Dante advances through the forest which covers it, and is guided towards the east by a young and fair lady (from whom he is separated by the river Lethe). There a marvelous procession defiles before his eyes, — seven lighted golden candlesticks, that, as they advance, tinge the air with the colors of the rainbow and form a canopy of light. Under this latter come twenty-four elders, clothed in white and crowned with lilies, and a triumphal car, drawn by a griffon, with the four animals described in Ezekiel and the Apocalypse at the corners, and seven nymphs on the sides (three on the right, and four on the left). Then

---

[1] [The unchaste, — the carnal sinners.]

come seven other elders crowned with purple flowers. When the car has come up to Dante, on the other side of the river, it stops at the reverberation of a clap of thunder; and he sees upon it, in a cloud of flowers thrown by hundreds of angels, Beatrice.

Dante recognizes her, feels the power of his ancient love, and turns awestruck to Vergil. But the latter has disappeared. There follow reproofs by Beatrice, sighs and tears by the poet, the relation of his straying, and his confessions, contrite and repentant. Then the lady who has guided him thus far plunges him into Lethe and so draws him to the opposite bank, giving him into the arms of the four nymphs on the left, who bring him before Beatrice. Thereupon the other three nymphs advance and obtain for Dante the joy of a glance from her and of her smile.

After this, all (including Dante and Statius) surround a "despoiled plant," and to it the griffon binds the car, causing the tree to become all green again. The poet sinks into a slumber, and upon awaking sees that the others have disappeared, and that Beatrice is seated upon the root of that tree, guarding the chariot, which is bound to it, and surrounded by the seven nymphs who care for the seven candlesticks. "For profit of the world which lives ill" she causes him to see various metamorphoses of the car itself and the outrage finally put upon it, and foretells its restoration to its primitive form through the efforts of one "sent by God"; and then, at last calling by name upon the lady who has guided the poet to her (Matilda), she tells her to lead Dante to the river Eunoe and to immerse him in it, reviving his spent power (as is her custom). Thus Dante becomes "pure and disposed to mount unto the stars."

5. Dante ascends through the heavens and attains the goal of his journey. And now we see Beatrice fix her eyes on the Sun (for we are in the third cantica), and Dante, gazing upon her, becomes transhumanized. He becomes aware of his extremely rapid ascent to heaven from the summit of the mountain by seeing this heaven illumined by the Sun, and like a lake of light. Having reached the heaven of the Moon, he obtains from his guide an explanation of the spots on this heavenly body, as well as of the " mirrored faces " of the souls who were *defective* on account of broken vows, and who appear to him here. At the suggestion of Beatrice he questions one of them, Piccarda Donati, and he discourses with his guide, who relieves him from several doubts.

In the second heaven (that of Mercury), among the spirits who were *active* through their desire for honor, that of Justinian comes to meet him. The latter, after having told the story of his own life, recounts that of the Roman empire. Beatrice, having resolved other doubts of the poet (about the justice and necessity of Christ's death), makes him ascend to the next heaven (that of Venus). Here Charles Martel, one of the spirits who whirl swiftly about in this heaven, reveals himself to Dante. The latter (after having obtained the assent of his guide, as always) converses profitably with him, and afterwards with Cunizza da Romano and Folco of Marseilles.

Upon entering the heaven of the Sun a garland of splendors surrounds his lady and himself, whirling about them three times. Among these *wise* spirits is Thomas Aquinas, who points out the others to him, and, in removing one of the doubts that he knows to have arisen in Dante's mind, narrates the life of St. Francis. Thereupon a new garland of spirits appears around the first, and one of these, Bonaventura da Bagnorea, points out the others to him and relates to him the life of St. Dominic.

After the solution of other questions Dante ascends in an instant to the fifth heaven (that of Mars). Here, within a luminous cross in the interior of that planet, he sees most vivid splendors moving swiftly from one point to another. Among these spirits *militant* through love for the faith, his great-great-grandfather appears benignly before him, and converses with him at great length, giving Dante information about himself, his family, and the Florence of former times, and exhorting him to tell without evasion what he has seen during his journey.

In the sixth heaven the poet is addressed by an eagle formed of the *just* spirits who governed rightly. This eagle instructs him on various points; and since two of the six spirits who form its eye are pagans, it explains their presence in Paradise. Then Dante mounts with his lady into the heaven of Saturn, where a golden ladder stretches up higher than the eye can reach. Dante, with the consent of Beatrice, questions to good profit two of the *contemplative* spirits, who are mounting and descending this ladder. These are St. Peter Damian and St. Benedict. Then, impelled by his lady, he mounts the ladder and comes into the Starry heaven, whence he can view the lower planets, as well as the habitable earth, and witness the triumph of Christ and the coronation of the Virgin. Then, at the request of Beatrice, St. Peter, St. James, and St. John examine the poet on faith, hope, and charity respectively. And having mounted to the ninth heaven, he sees God in the form of a point of light, with the nine angelic orders revolving swiftly around Him. Beatrice gives him the most minute and ample explanation as regards these latter.

In the meantime her beauty increases indescribably, and Dante finally finds himself in the Empyrean. The "pure white rose" of the city of God appears to him; and in place of Beatrice the poet now becomes aware that he is standing beside St. Bernard, the Contemplator, whom she herself has sent to him. Dante takes leave of his lady afar off, who is seated on her proper throne. And the holy elder points out to him the Virgin and the souls most worthy of note, explaining to him briefly the structure of the heavenly rose. At this point he obtains from the Madonna the grace to raise his eyes higher towards the Ultimate Salvation, so that "the Supreme Pleasure may be displayed to him." And Dante may finally see and contemplate God.

CHAPTER IV

THE "TRUE": "HIDDEN TRUTH" OR ALLEGORY

I. SCENE OF THE REAL ACTION. 1. Consideration of the sins and punishments. 2. Justification and glorification.

II. THE REAL ACTION. 1. Dante comes to his senses, is "hindered" in his conversion, and is helped. 2. Is progressively redeemed from the slavery of sin. 3. Fixes his mind upon the pursuit of the state of righteousness (*justitia*). 4. Revives his "spent power" and rises in his speculations even to the contemplation of God (*gloria*).

I. SCENE OF THE REAL ACTION

1. Consideration of the sins and punishments. The subject of the *Commedia*, that is, the liberation of the author from the wood and from the wild beasts by means of a journey through the otherworld, is imagery. On the other hand, the truth (as Dante himself would have us believe) is the passing of his soul from a disorderly disposition to salvation. And following out this idea, the regions through which he imagines himself as going, correspond to successive states through which his soul has passed. The scene of the imaginary action is a symbol of the scene of the real action. Let us see in what way.[1]

The valley, the slope, and the mountain, which Dante puts before us at the beginning of his work, symbolize respectively the *state of misery inherent in the vicious life*, the *state of transition* the *state of felicity inherent in the virtuous life*.

[1] The reasons for the following allegorical interpretation may be found fully treated in my *Significati*, part ii, chap. 1.

In the state of transition we mount unconsciously toward Good, drawn by the light of the renascent *natural love* or *upright love* (the Sun), which tends to it. The " true " way (up over the mountain) and the " not true," [1] which is the opposite of it (down along the valley), taken together offer us an imaginary representation of the *moral progress of man*. So far as regards the end for which man is ordained by his Maker, in the *vicious life* (the wooded incline of the valley) this progress descends ; in the intermediate state (the " slope ") it is slightly inclined ; [2] in the *virtuous life* (the " steep ") it mounts. The way up the mountain is *virtuous activity*, that along the valley is *vicious activity*.

The underground continuation of the second of these ways is that which traverses from top to bottom the " eternal place," where the damned have their abode. This sole way of escape from the " savage place " [3] signifies, as regards the real action there carried out (that is, the spiritual journey through it), *vicious activity inasmuch as it, in its essence and in the effects which proceed from it to all eternity, is revealed to us by the light granted us for this end.*[4] Just as Hell (which is traversed by this

---

[1] Cf. *Purg.* xxx, 130.

[2] We must remember the insensible inclination of the slope. In this state man inclines toward good or evil, without actually doing either.

[3] Cf. *Inf.* i, 93.

[4] Vergil. " And who is this that shows the road ? " Brunetto Latini asks Dante (*Inf.* xv, 48). The poet replies, " This one appeared to me . . . and he is leading me homeward again along this path."

road), that is, the subterranean valley corresponding to the one which contains the wood, is, in the allegory of the poem, *the state of misery inherent in the vicious life, inasmuch as it, in the causes which determine it and in the various forms which it assumes to all eternity, is revealed to us by the aforesaid light.*

If we accept this view, the visit to the " eternal prison " of the damned, which is the only means of salvation for the souls who are captives of sin while alive,[1] signifies in all probability *the wise and careful consideration, in the light of the guide*[2] *which is granted us by Providence for that end, of the vicious activity in its methods, its roots, and in the "endlessly bitter" effects which proceed from it.* The mind must of necessity create these latter effects in its imagination, in accord with the suggestions of reason and observation.[3] The methods and the roots it must work out according to the philosophical doctrines (*philosophica documenta*) imparted by human reason, and based on the foundation of that part of the " Ethics " of the master of reason itself — Aristotle — which treats of the vices.

It is clear that the obstacles which are met in such a visit to the realm of damnation, and which result from its structure or from its devilish ministers, must, if the visit itself represent the aforesaid spiritual meaning, have their own individual symbolic signification, which applies to the soul making this visit. Let us see what they are.

---

[1] Cf. *Purg.* xxx, 136–138 (" . . . all means for his salvation were already short, save showing him the lost people ").   [2] Vergil.

[3] That is as much as to say that, as far as these effects are concerned, the truth which may be known is only an individual imagery ; that hence Dante, when he describes the punishments of the damned and their various states, hides no allegory under the literal meaning.

We have already said that vicious activity is the object of our consideration. Now, according to the "Ethics" of the Master and the "Commentary" of St. Thomas, two things in the soul are the beginning of such activity, namely, evil *passions* and perverted *habits*. The former are to be recognized in the rivers of the abyss, the latter in the monsters. The "course" of the "tears," flowing out from the fissure by which all the parts of the Old Man of Crete are cleft except his head,[1] "which is from rock to rock" down through the infernal valley even to its depth, represents the disorderly movement of the sensuous appetite, to which man is subject since the corrupt state[2] succeeded to the original pure state[3] (by the *vulneratio naturae*).[4] This is, then, in so far as it is the cause of man's misery, *human passion* in its various forms; that is, the *movement of the sensuous concupiscent appetite* (Acheron), the *movement of the sensuous irascible appetite* (Styx), and the *movement of the sensuous appetite* (*concupiscent and irascible*) *denaturalized by the perverted will*[5] *so as to become disorderly after the fashion of the beasts* (Phlegethon), or *so as to hold oneself back by the*

---

[1] See above, pp. 36–37; and cf. *Inf.* xiv, 103–114.

[2] The Old Man of Crete is *man in his moral state through the ages*. The powers of his soul naturally ordered by virtue, that is, reason and will (*vires superiores*), are to be found in the two parts of the Old Man "down to the fork," — one of silver and the other of brass. And the sensuous appetite, divided into the concupiscent and irascible, is in the lower twofold division, all of iron, but with one foot (that is, one of the *moral fundamentals*) of terra-cotta, which denotes the fragility of the concupiscent, on which man leans the more, notwithstanding.

[3] This state is typified by the head of the Old Man, which is "of fine gold" and not cleft by a fissure.

[4] Cf. St. Thomas Aquinas, *Summa theologica*, pars 1 ii^ae, quaest. 85, art. 3. This *vulneratio* is extremely well indicated by the aforesaid fissure.

[5] The perverted will, or *desire for evil*, is represented by the fiery wall of the city of Dis, through which the infernal waters pass.

The Old Man of Crete

(Man in his moral state through the ages)

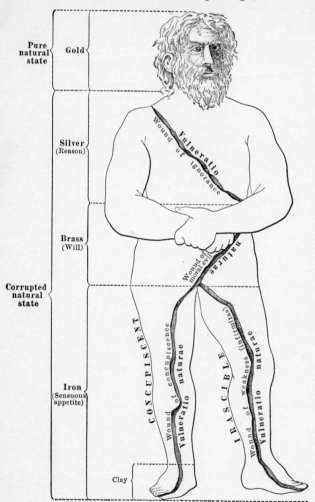

effect of diabolic withdrawal from every "heat of love" (Cocytus). Thus the "course" of the "tears" down through the valley of the abyss corresponds to the " stream " down through the wooded valley.[1] And, in truth, this is no other than the *fluctus cupiditatum*,[2] — the disorderly movement of the lower forces of the soul, which sweep it away to damnation.

As the rivers of Hell are the evil passions, so the monsters are the perverted habits of *concupiscence* (Charon), *gluttony* (Cerberus), *evil spending* (Plutus), *wrath* (Phlegyas), *violence* (the Minotaur), *fraud* (Geryon). Minos represents the *divine punitive justice in so far as there is admonition;* the devils, who in their distinctive forms guard the entrance to Dis, and are deputed to govern the fifth ditch of Malebolge, signify the *diabolic temptations in general, and especially those of fraud;* the Centaurs symbolize the *violent bestial temptations;* the Giants, the *temptations to rebellion against natural order.*

As for the Furies who threaten to petrify Dante from the top of a tower on the walls of Dis, these ministers of *diabolic envy* (Hecate, " queen of eternal wailing ") are the *mad appetite for injury*, which, by means of the *habit of injury* itself (Medusa), produces that hardness of heart[3] by which man becomes the eternal prisoner of obstinate *desire for evil* (the walls of Dis).

2. Justification and glorification. We give now the most probable allegorical meaning of the other regions which we have seen to constitute the scene of the imaginary action, that is, of the places which Dante pictures himself as visiting after Hell.

---

[1] See above, pp. 34–35.   [2] Cf. *De monarchia*, iii, 16.
[3] This is the *obduratio cordis* of the theologians.

The " hidden path," by which we mount from the center of the earth to the hemisphere opposite ours, symbolizes that part of the way of salvation in which the soul, having meditated on evil, gradually draws away from every thought which is connected with this evil.   The inclined plain

The Abyss of vice
considered in the light of right reason

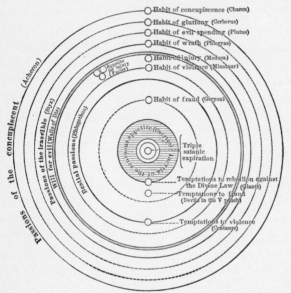

around the mountain of the Earthly Paradise (where this path debouches) is *the state of the soul which has come forth from the slavery of sin and seeks a means of rising to the felicity of activity according to virtue.* This means is figured by the " passage " which leads up the mountain to the " summit " occupied by the garden where " man is happy," [1] that is, leaving out the imagery, to the felicity

[1] *Purg.* xxx, 75.

alluded to above. The "noble" faculty of the mind which counsels and points out that means is impersonated by Cato, who rules over all the ascent of the mountain from the plain which surrounds it. He is, then, the discernment of selection, which is not hampered and is turned in the right direction, that is, *free will*.[1] The habit by whose grace we advance in right activity, and hence also in the felicity which proceeds from it, is impersonated by Matilda, who, on the table-land on the top of the mountain, is the guide for those who would visit the garden which covers it. She is then the principle from which spring all the moral virtues "which *make* man happy in his activity," [2] that is, the *habit of our good selection*.[3]

But in what does the aforesaid *means* consist? What is the symbolism of the fatiguing path from the "country" at the foot of the mountain (whose meaning we know) to the "holy country" on its summit, that is, to the state of felicity consisting in the activity of one's own virtue? It symbolizes *justification* — the movement of the soul to the attainment of the state of righteousness (*justitia*) — in its successive stages, that of the *preparation for justifying grace* and that of the *remission of sins* (by means of the influx of grace itself and the removal of evil habits). The first of these stages, during which the will is strengthened as regards penitence by the consideration of the *poena damni*, which those who neglected their repentance suffer in the otherworld, is fittingly figured by the "hillside where one waits," [4] which is their assigned place. The

---

[1] Cf. *Purg.* xviii, 73–74 ("this noble faculty Beatrice understands as free will").   [2] Cf. *Conv.* ode iii, stanza 5.

[3] *Conv.* treatise iv, chap. 17. It will be remembered that Matilda is going " [choosing] flower from flower" (*Purg.* xxviii, 41).

[4] *Purg.* xxiii, 89.

second, during which the will becomes free and sane, thanks to the "purity" which is gained there by considering the *poena sensus*, which is suffered by many of those who, nevertheless, do not die in the wrath of God, is figured, no less fittingly, by the "seven realms" of Cato, that is to say, the seven ledges where the spirits are purified while they dwell "in torments." The transition from one to the other, that is, the admission to salvation by the angelic executor of the Divine Care [1] by means of the remission of sins, is symbolized by the gate to the kingdom of heaven,[2] and by its opening through the action of an angel assigned to inculcate penitence.[3]

Finally, as the steep of the "holy mountain" represents *justification* in its various steps, which justification leads to the *state of felicity inherent in the virtuous life* (Earthly Paradise), in the knowledge of which the *habit of good selection* (Matilda) makes us advance, just so the "stairs of the eternal palace," [4] that is, the nine concentric heavens which are contained within the Empyrean, represent *glorification* in its various steps, which leads to the *state of felicity consisting in the fruition of the "divine aspect"* (Celestial Paradise or Empyrean), in the knowledge of which the *habit of contemplation* (St. Bernard, the "Contemplator") makes us advance. And this is attained, thanks

[1] In such things do we find the *guardianship of the angels*. And what can help our eternal salvation more than divine inspiration through our guardian angel?

[2] The three steps leading to this gate (see above, p. 60) signify, beginning with the lowest, the *consciousness of our moral state*, the *contrition for such a state*, and the *fervent and steadfast love of good*. To the latter there is added immediately the *purpose to persevere in good*, represented by the sill of adamant to the gate itself, that is, of *conversion to good by means of penitence*, which gives entrance to the remission of sins.

[3] Penitence is treated here as a virtue, not as a sacrament.

[4] *Parad.* xxi, 7–8.

to speculative activity. The highest point of beatitude which is attainable in the life of man is that of the vision of God "in his essence," which not even faith can obtain for us. The habit of contemplation alone can procure for us from God such a supreme revelation.

So, passing finally from the state of attained *righteousness* to that of complete *glory*, the way of salvation, along which we shall now see the true action of the poem develop, terminates in a momentary state of beatitude, which is a true "first fruit" of the Eternal Pleasure.

II. The Real Action

1. Dante comes to his senses, is "hindered" in his conversion, and is helped. Dante's soul (whose passing through the various moral states mentioned up to this point is shadowed forth by the imaginary journey of the poet in flesh and blood) was in his youth rightly disposed [1] and strengthened in his right intention by that highest of all earthly pleasures which came to him at the sight of the fair body of Bice. For the beauty which attracted his love — an imprint of the Divine Beauty, shining through this body — led Dante's soul, after having turned it in the right direction, towards the source of every "true light," towards the Highest Good. When Beatrice had disappeared from this world, Dante's soul, no longer guided by the light of truth radiating from "the youthful eyes," had fallen, *aversa a divino lumine*, into the dark places of error and sin, evilly disposed now in his mind as well as in his affections.

These are the antecedents of the real action, and are furnished by the letter of the poem. The real action itself,

[1] Cf. *Purg.* xxx, 109–117.

hidden under the veil of the imaginary, may be resumed
as follows :

At the age of thirty-five, after ten years' wandering, the
poet becomes more acutely aware of his own misery, and
turning anew from his false love to the true, he again
looks upon the "height" of habitual virtuous action, as
upon a not deceptive object of our instinctive desire for
felicity. And he advances towards this "height," unconsciously nearing the good. But at the very moment when
he is about to mount to Heaven by means of right activity,
a threefold "hindrance" stops him. It is the disposition to
evil, or "infirmity," contracted during his sojourn in vice,
which opposes itself to him in its three aspects ; and first
in that of moral evil pure and simple (*the she-leopard*),
which "incurs more blame," but is less to be feared for
the soul which may again expand in the rays of the love
of God. Dante's soul is hindered by this moral evil in its
return towards that Good which is the aim of man. But
though it is turned from its just intention by this obstacle,
nevertheless (thanks to its unfolding in the rays of divine
love, and to the consequent reawakening of its good
instincts) [1] it does not despair of subduing the animal by
means of the command of the will over the perverted
habits, with which command it is provided, however imperfect it may be (*the cord*).[2]

But here his mortal "infirmity" opposes itself to him
under two other aspects : that of bestial moral evil or "mad
bestiality," greedily and irrationally violent (*the lion*) ; and
that of moral evil arising from passion or "incontinence,"
which excites every kind of disorderly appetite (*the she-wolf*).

---

[1] " The hour of the time and the sweet season" (cf. *Inf*. i, 37–42).
[2] Cf. *Inf*. xvi, 106–108.

Under this last aspect (which is less displeasing to God,[1] but far more to be feared, because the will to do good does not suffice against it) the moral evil or infirmity, which has been acquired, discourages the poet's soul to such a degree that it despairs of ever being able to attain the mark at which it is aiming, and it is again on the point of being turned back to perdition by its perverted appetites.

And now comes the aid, since the relapse is involuntary. To Dante's soul, which has retraced in great distress the interval between the life of virtue and that of vice, and stands upon the edge of the abyss looking back upon evil,[2] there appears, by heavenly will, to check it as it is rushing headlong down, reason as it was in the " good world " when God brought himself to grant to men their " bringer of beatitude " (the Christian Faith). This is right reason (*Vergil*), which alone can raise us (by persuading us and demonstrating to us) to the felicity of acting according to one's own virtue. Its voice at first comes faintly to the soul no longer accustomed to hear it.[3] But very soon, after having invoked its aid, the soul can receive its counsels. And right reason, having made the soul confess that its own strength is not sufficient to enable it to conquer the formidable obstacle of the evil disposition of incontinence, warns it that, even with the aid of this same reason, it would in vain essay again the short ascent to the eagerly desired felicity by means of good activities. For that very grievous infirmity through which man is a slave of his insatiable appetites, from the time when the envy of the devil

[1] The *moral evil* which " acquires hate in heaven " is (as we know) the bestial and, even to a greater extent, moral evil pure and simple.

[2] Cf. *Parad*. xxxii, 138 (" when thou didst bend thy brow to rush downward ").

[3] " Who appeared faint-voiced through long silence " (*Inf*. i, 63).

made him subject to such disorder by leading him on to his first sin, will hinder his soul at every point. There is only one way of escape, long and difficult, — that of considering very minutely in the light of this right reason the " state of infelicity inherent in the vicious life," both in the causes that determine it (*the sins*) and in the forms which it assumes, either temporarily or to eternity (*the punishments*). The poet's soul consents to start on such a path, but later, assailed by a sense of unworthiness, it fears that it is too presuming. Then right reason reassures his soul, showing it how the true light may come to it from the Divine Care (*the "three blessed ladies" who care for Dante in heaven*). For, at the instigation of divine pity (*the "gentle lady" — Mary*), the power of God to make righteous the guilty (*Lucia*) by means of the supernatural truth which makes man blessed (*Beatrice*) [1] has sent to enlighten his soul that reason, which has miraculously returned for a short moment just as it was when the " good Augustus " ruled the " good world " in peace.

After this Dante's soul goes deeply into that salutary meditation upon the sins and their punishments, according to the philosophic teachings of right reason, which is to say, according to the " Ethics " of Aristotle, " master and leader of human reason, inasmuch as [it looks toward] its conclusive activity." [2]

2. Dante is progressively redeemed from the slavery of sin. As a first step his soul considers the sin and punishment of the pusillanimous. These will remain to eternity in the " country " which surrounds the infernal pit,

---

[1] As we see, the Divine Care (on which see *De vulgari eloquentia*, ed. Rajna, p. 8, and St. Thomas, *Summa theologica*, pars. 1, quaest. 22, art. 1) corresponds in its three aspects to the three essential attributes of God, — love, power, and wisdom. [2] *Conv.* treatise iv, chap. 6.

set apart both from those expiating their sins on the mountain and the damned in the valley. This is because they have lived in the " intermediate state between vice and virtue " (*the deserted slope*) averse to God, without doing, although able, that which they ought to have done in conformity with the sign given them by God.[1] His soul then fixes its attention upon the precipitate rush of the vast mob towards the passions of the concupiscent appetite, which condemn them (*the Acheron*), and upon the habit of concupiscence [luxury] (*Charon*), the oldest of all habits which lead men to perdition. Right reason then, continuing the consideration of the first grade of the abyss of vice, which is constituted by unbelief pure and simple, penetrates the concept of our natural nobility (*the* "*noble castle*"), recalling the worth of fame ever green (*the* "*green enamel*" *which welcomes the* "*great spirits*"). After which, at the moment of undertaking the consideration of the truly evil acts according to the order of their increasing gravity, it meditates upon avenging divine justice considered in its process (*Minos*).

Luxury is the first of the sins proceeding from infirmity or moral evil of the soul " arising from passion," that is, from incontinence, which presents itself to Dante's mind. Inclined to love, and yet reflecting upon the terrible struggle between the powerful inclinations of nature and the austerity of human and divine law, the poet's soul is disturbed and remains dismayed. Reason hastens to draw it away from such dismal considerations, and puts successively before it the habit of gluttony (*Cerberus*) and the manner of punishment which befits those guilty of this

[1] *The ensign*, which, for their punishment, these people must follow without ever being able to overtake it (cf. *Inf.* iii, 52–57).

sin; the habit of evil spending (*Plutus*) and the appropriate punishment for the perverted use of money; the habit of wrath (*Phlegyas*) and the sad effects of fury, of rancor, and of *tumor animi*,[1] that is, of the passions of the irascible appetite (*Styx*), which contaminate and make sullen.

Guided, as always, by right reason, Dante's soul makes ready now to penetrate the secrets of that moral evil, which, since it does not arise from passion but from choice, acquires hate in heaven. It sees that not even right reason suffices of itself to triumph over the powers of hell, which are bent on hindering our passing, for our own salvation, to the consideration of the most grave sins comprised in the enclosure of obstinate will for evil inflamed by hate (*the walls of the city of Dis*). And there presents itself to his mind the mad appetite for injury, corresponding in its threefold aspect to the three kinds of " evil wrath " whence it proceeds (*the Furies*), which is the means whereby diabolic envy (*the "queen of eternal wailing"*) renders us subject to the habit of injury (*Medusa*) which hardens the heart forever.

Having conquered the diabolic resistance, thanks to the angelic guard, executor of the Divine Care (*the angel "sent from Heaven"*), Dante's soul can finally scrutinize minutely moral evil " from choice," beginning with heresy, comprehended in the aforesaid enclosure of the will for evil, but still without forming part of the last abyss of vice. Right reason explains to it, according to the Aristotelian "Ethics," the divisions and the subdivisions of human moral evil, both that which " incurs less blame," which has been already considered, as well as the other " which acquires hate in heaven," now taken under consideration. Thus the poet's soul, penetrating more deeply into the

---

[1] [I have elsewhere (p. 42) translated this " inflation of mind."]

investigation of the uttermost pit of evil, can now see in the light of right reason both the habit of violence (*the Minotaur*), generated by " bestiality " and the bestial passions, that is, " blind cupidity " and " mad anger " (*Phlegethon*), and the violent bestial temptations (*the Centaurs*), who prick with sharp goads those who are immersed in such passions. And finally it sees the various forms of bestial moral evil or bestiality, with the punishments proper to them. Right reason explains to it the origin of all the evil passions by the morally corrupt state of man, which has succeeded to the pure natural state (*the Old Man of Crete*). Whereupon, having finished its consideration of bestial moral evil and preparing to explore the secrets of moral evil pure and simple (which is the worst), right reason causes to be entrusted to itself, in order that this may be wholly under its own control, the command (albeit still imperfect) of the will over the perverted habits (*the cord*). It was with this that Dante's soul, when it instinctively turned back alone towards Good, had tried to restrain the disposition to moral evil pure and simple; and it now makes use of this to call up before it the habit of fraud (*Geryon*) whence spring the acts of that moral evil, so that this habit may be known without danger.

In this manner Dante's soul, following with the intellect the process of fraudulent activity (*Geryon's course down through the pit*), descends to consider the horrible punishments befitting the basest degradation of human moral evil enslaved by the diabolic. Great assistance comes continually to the poet's soul in this examination from right reason, to whose guidance it not infrequently entrusts itself entirely. This reason shows it the dangers of the diabolic temptations to fraud (*the Malebranche*), leads it to consider at close range the sin of hypocrisy, and shows it how much labor it costs to free oneself from this hypocrisy. And so, having examined the sins of that moral evil which is intent on injuring with fraud those who put no particular trust in the one who does the harm, the poet's soul passes on to consider those sins of that moral evil which is intent on injuring those who put personal trust in the ones who do the evil. And so there present themselves to the mind the temptations to rebellion against the natural order established by God (*the Giants*). And following the line of thought suggested by these, with its mind firmly fixed on reason (its guide), the soul can sound, in its meditations, the depth of human depravity (*the " depth " in which Antæus places the two poets*), where such temptations cause to fall headlong any one who seconds them with his will.[1] And here it can see the course of the sensuous appetite checked by the total withdrawal from the heat of love (*the " ice " of Cocytus*), and its derivation from the malignant exhalation from the Primal Evil (against which there is no other protection than right reason).[2] Finally, reason shows to the poet's soul this inhuman monster in all its frightful ugliness, — the perfect antitype of the Trinity, which is love, wisdom, and power, — in its three aspects of moral evil, ignorance, and impotence (*the three faces of Lucifer, — red, black, and " between white and yellow "*). And it shows his soul how this malignant exhalation is threefold (through the very effect of this triform nature), just as we see to be threefold the evil disposition or *moral evil*, that is, " infirmity," to which man is subject from the fall of our first parents, and according to which his sins are classified. And so we

[1] Cf. *Inf.* xi, 61–63.   [2] Cf. *Inf.* xxxiv, 8–9.

find the origin of the " hindrance " which was met by Dante's soul in its return to the life of virtue, as well as the infinite bitterness tasted in the life of vice : from the moral evil, from the ignorance, and from the impotence of the devil comes the moral evil, the bestiality, and the incontinence of man. The " way not true " leads to this supreme misery whence his straying proceeds.

Now Dante's soul, healed from the infirmity which has hindered it from mounting up over the abandoned true way, can finally withdraw from the consideration of the abyss of misery into which man is precipitated in his pursuit of the false images of good ; can return in search of the good which does not deceive, of the felicity which does not lie.

3. Dante fixes his mind upon the pursuit of the state of righteousness. Having come forth from the slavery of sin, and having returned to where he may see the cardinal virtues (the four stars), his soul continues in its submission to reason. And the latter, following the counsels of free will (*Cato*), provides his will with *a command over perverted habits, which is susceptible to every impulse of righteous appetite* (the reed), after having cleared from every earthly disturbance [1] his perception, now ready to be turned upon celestial things. And the consideration of heavenly things begins at once ; for the poet's soul can contemplate immediately the splendor of the glory of the angels.[2] Thereupon, reflecting that he who has turned to God only at the last moment, and hence dies in a state similar to that in which his own soul was upon its first and unsuccessful emergence from a state of sin (*the deserted slope*), must expiate on the slope around the mountain

---

[1] Cf. *Purg.* i, 95–99.   [2] Cf. *Purg.* ii, 13–39.

["where reason scrutinizes us"][1] that presumption which
has made him disdain the light of grace until the very
last; reflecting thus the poet's soul entrusts itself to the
light of divine love (*the Sun*), and finds access to the way
of justification. It then proceeds along this latter, while
reason, preparing it for justifying grace, maintains its will
firmly fixed on "righteousness to the end." And, while
thinking on the *poena damni* which will be suffered in the
otherworld by those who have delayed their repentance
(who are set afar off, before "going to the punishments,"
on the ascent which corresponds to the first step in justification, beyond which they did not go in life), it continues
strengthening itself in its resolution for repentance. There
follows one of those halts[2] which, according to natural
law, alternate with the impulses of divine love in the sinner who is trying to mend. During this halt Dante's soul
not only considers the temporary state of the princes guilty
of negligence, although they had died at peace with God,
but it also lays hold of the necessity of invoking by prayer
the aid of heavenly pity, on the part of the sinner who is
intent on preparing himself for the remission of sins.[3]

In the meantime, in place of the cardinal virtues, the
theological present themselves to his soul; and the justifying virtue of Divine Care (*Lucia*) makes easy for this soul
the way which leads to the attainment of the state of righteousness. Thus, thanks to the renewed impulse of divine

[1] Here, as has been said, we find those who died repentant, but in
contumacy of the church.

[2] These are allegorically signified by the impossibility of ascending
the mountain after sunset.

[3] This is signified by the prayer to God by one of the souls who are
preparing themselves for penitence in the flowering valley, and by the
subsequent arrival of two angels sent by the Madonna, who put to flight
the insidious serpent.

love (*the newly arisen Sun*), it can attain salvation (*the gate of the kingdom of the heavens, which is at the same time the gate of Purgatory*). And the guardian angel, whose duty it is to inculcate the virtue of repentance, can invite it to advance to the remission of sins by passing over the three successive steps that we have already considered.[1] Then, in the measure that Dante's soul progressively considers the punishments proper for the expiation of each one of the seven mortal sins, Divine Care (by means of one of the celestial executors of its own will) cancels successively the marks of these sins (*the seven wounds, the seven P's imprinted on Dante's forehead*); and there is presented to the imagination sublime examples, either of the corresponding virtue or of punishments inflicted on those guilty of such vices. In such a manner the poet's soul mounts by the various grades of the aforesaid remission (the second degree of its *justification*), attaining at each one the "beatitude" corresponding to the sin which is purged. It purges itself first from the sins consequent on love perverted to evil or turned to good with less care than it ought, afterward from those consequent on love which abandons itself too strongly to fallacious good, of which latter good it has a vision pregnant with moral instruction (*the stammering woman*).[2] In this ascent it has finally as guide, together with reason as it was in the "good world" not yet converted to the new faith (*Vergil*), reason as it was in one who had already become a Christian (*Statius*). Whence it can meditate, in the light of its new guide, on the highest truths of the natural order, and, assisted by both, boldly face the punishment of the mortification of the flesh (*the passage*

---

[1] See pp. 60 and 75.   [2] *Purg.* xix, 1–33.

through the fire). After this it has the vision of what it is on the point of attaining, — habitual activity in good (*Leah*), the source of true felicity in this world ; and this felicity is soon after foretold it by right reason, which, having conducted it in this manner to the "height," previously longed for in vain, has fulfilled its office and carried out its promise.

4. Dante revives his " spent power " and rises in his speculations even to the contemplation of God. After having considered the eternal and the temporal punishments, and having the remains of sin removed, Dante's soul has now come to the third and last step in the justification obtained through the Divine Care (that is, to habitual activity in good). And, desirous of acquiring experience of the active life in virtue (*the "divine forest dense and living"*), it proceeds through the state of felicity to which right reason has raised it by its teachings (*the table-land on the mountain*). The habitual choice of good (*Matilda*), the beginning of every moral virtue, appears before it, charming and attractive, as one whose duty it is to make us enjoy all the pleasures of the state of earthly felicity, consisting in the activity of our own virtue. As yet the poet's soul cannot attain this ardently desired habit; there is between them the unattained forgetfulness of the sins which were committed (*Lethe*). Nevertheless, while proceeding in this direction, it advances so far "in the straight way " that there again shines before it that supernatural light that came to it, awakening its love, from the youthful eyes of the woman-miracle. The Truth " which so high exalts us," the Supernatural Truth necessary to us, granted man for his salvation by the Holy Spirit by means of the Prophets and Hagiographers, of

Jesus Christ, and of his disciples,[1] appears before his soul then in all the glory of its *triumph* — composed of the seven gifts of the Holy Spirit (*the seven candlesticks*), the books of the Prophets and Hagiographers (*the twenty-four elders*), Jesus Christ (*the griffon*), and the books of his disciples (*the four animals and the last seven old men*) — having for its depositary and dispenser the Church of Rome (*the triumphal car*). This Truth, that is, the Christian Faith, is its "bringer of beatitude"; it now replaces reason as the guide in what remains to be done, that is, in the contemplation of the divine things.[2] And at its tribunal,[3] with solemn show of penitence, the poet's soul confesses that it has sinned in turning away from the true good, which had been shown it by the woman-miracle, in order to seek after the false good; it shows its own sincere contrition; it realizes the great difference between the attraction of transitory things and the incomparable beauty of Eternal Truth. Then the habit (at last attained) of the choice of good can lead it, through the forgetfulness of sins already remitted and now absolved (*Lethe*), to the practice of the cardinal virtues (*the ladies on the left of the car*), which in their turn lead it to consider close at hand that Truth which the Word incarnate " brought to earth " (*Beatrice*).[4] And from the latter, thanks to the three higher virtues, the theological (*the ladies on the right of the car*), the poet's soul finally obtains the joy of her demonstrations and persuasions (*the eyes and the mouth of Beatrice*), longed for in vain for ten years. And she, that is, the Christian Faith, causes it to attain, by

[1] These are the words of Dante himself at the end of the *De monarchia*, which are so often quoted.

[2] This is why Vergil disappears at the coming of Beatrice.

[3] The *car*, that is, the Church.   [4] Cf. *Parad.* loc. cit.

means of the habitual choice of good, the revivification of
the memory of every good deed (*Eunoe*) and, at the same
time, of its spent power, its "disposition — formerly
hindered by the habits of evil — to contemplate heavenly
things."

Thus, pure and disposed to good,[1] Dante's soul mounts,
following the demonstrations of Revealed Truth (*Beatrice's eyes*), to consider these things in his speculations.
After the completion of its justification it passes on immediately to the attainment of holiness; then, by means
of the natural love of the Highest Good (*the Sun*), cor-
roborated by Faith (*Beatrice*), the "Love that governs
heaven"[2] raises it, by making it turn away from the ap-
prehension of the things of sense (*the transhumanizing of
the poet*), to a loftier contemplation of that which, when
revealed, constitutes the object of the beatitude of the
Saints. Then follows its intellectual movement from object to object, ever higher and higher (*the ascent through
the heavens*), in which movement is comprised the greatest
participation in the heavenly glory in this world, and by
means of which Dante can contemplate spiritually the
grades of blessedness, one by one, and can propound, and
often resolve, grave theological questions, according to
the teachings which Revealed Truth imparts in various
ways.[3] By virtue of this the poet's soul rises hence by
means of the contemplative activity of the intellect (*the
"golden stairway" which starts from the heaven of the
contemplative*) even to the point of being able to form an

---

[1] Cf. the last verse of the second cantica.   [2] *Parad.* i, 74.

[3] These are the *documenta spiritualia quae humanam rationem trans-
cendunt*, the *rivelata*, by means of which we attain the blessedness of
eternal life, which consists in the fruition of the divine aspect (see the
close of the *De monarchia*).

idea of the triumph of Christ and the coronation of the Virgin. And since in the demonstrations of this Truth there arises the reflection of the image of God, in so far as He is the mover of the universe, the soul can also look upon Him in His relations with the universe itself. Finally, upon turning to the contemplation of the Empyrean, the goal of its advancement to glory, Dante's soul sees the supreme splendor of the beauty of Revealed Truth, of the Christian Faith. And the latter has fulfilled its office as guide. His soul can succeed in discerning spiritually the details of the celestial court only through the merit of the habit of contemplation (*St. Bernard the "Contemplator"*), which Faith itself has provided for his soul, and which will obtain for it at last the unprecedented grace of seeing God, in a spiritual rapture, as the blessed see Him.

CHAPTER V

THE "SUPERSENSE," OR ANAGOGE, AND THE HIDDEN AND MANIFEST "DOCTRINE"

1. The anagogic action. 2. The hidden "doctrine" and the ultimate end of the threefold action (*imaginary, allegorical, anagogic*). 3. The manifest "doctrine": the sciences of the Trivium in the *Commedia*. 4. The sciences of the Quadrivium: the astronomical details and the data of the Dantesque journey. 5. How the doctrinal elements are blended with the artistic in the *Commedia*.

1. The anagogic action, or "supersense." According to the concept which Dante had, as we know, of the anagogic sense, or "supersense," we may deduce another and loftier truth by starting from the hidden truth or allegory, with which we have dealt up to this point, and raising it to a meaning which shall refer to "supernal things." The story of the poet's soul redeemed from its *disposition to evil* and admitted to *justification* and *glory* is the story of the human soul redeemed from its long infirmity and restored to Purgatory and the Celestial Paradise.

In Eden, where it passed its *early life*,[1] the human soul was disposed to good and strengthened in its right intention by the love which was inspired in it by the beauty of Supernatural Truth, whose needful demonstrations (*the "youthful eyes" of Beatrice*) were granted it by Divine Care. When sin came, this soul was turned aside "from the way of truth and from its own life,"[2] continually plunging deeper into the abyss of error (*the valley with "the dark wood"*). But near the time that "all Heaven

---

[1] [*Vita nova*.]   [2] *Parad.* vii, 39.

willed to bring the world to its own serene mood,"[1] having gained the consciousness of its own unhappy state,
the human soul begins to feel the sincere, albeit vain,
desire to issue forth from it. Then Divine Care, in its
pity, puts its hand to the work of the redemption of this
soul. And it first makes provision for overcoming the
"hindrance" of its threefold disposition to evil or "infirmity" (*the three wild beasts*), by means of pure and
right reason, which reveals to this soul the way of meditation on evil deeds in the order of their increasing gravity
(*the visit to the "lost peoples"*) ; that is to say, by means
of such a use of the "Ethics" — the only means of freeing
oneself from the slavery of sin, before the revelation of
the new Faith — as to permit of its detesting, through
the knowledge that it acquires of them, both evil passions
and perverted habits, and, above all, those three dispositions whence proceed all evil activities.

By these philosophic teachings of reason,[2] that is to say,
thanks to the doctrine of the Peripatetics, which had come
to be considered as "almost Catholic,"[3] the human soul,
now near to being restored to the glory of the heavens by
means of the spiritual teachings of the new Faith, its
bringer of beatitude,[4] obtains from Divine Care the grace
of healing itself from its own threefold disposition to evil.

[1] Cf. *Parad*. vi, 55–56. Then, under the first "standard-bearer" who,
by will of Rome, should take upon himself to exercise the imperial authority, the world began to have right reason [*Vergil*] (" I was born *sub
Julio*, though late "). This would fully explain its virtue "under the
good Augustus," in the fullness of time (*plenitudo temporum*).

[2] The *philosophica documenta, ostensa nobis ab humana ratione* (see
the end of the *De monarchia*).

[3] *Conv*. treatise iv, chap. 6. We have already seen that Aristotle was
for Dante the "master of human reason."

[4] The *documenta spiritualia ostensa a Spiritu Sancto* (see the above-
cited passage in the *De monarchia*).

For the study of the " Ethics" conclusively teaches it that
its infirmity proceeds from a corruption of human nature.
This latter was originally pure, as it was in the world which
was ruled by its " illustrious leader," Saturn, "under whom
all wickedness lay dead " ; [1] and as it may be again if all
civilization will only look to Rome "as its mirror," that
city which is destined to restore the "good world," ruled
and regulated by a new leader, the Emperor.[2]

And this is how, "*sub divo Augusto,* when there was
a perfect monarchy," [3] human beings — thanks to right
reason in the fullness of time (*Vergil, who lived " in Rome
under the good Augusto "*) — are again *conversi ad bo-
num* and are in sight of Heaven, to which they naturally
tend.[4] They are in the way of aiming at the acquisition
of the moral virtues (*the " four stars, never seen save by
the first people "*) which, in the midst of an as yet pagan
society, obtained for Cato his final salvation ; and of beginning their justification (*the ascent of the mountain*),
that is, the return to the state of original righteousness
(*the Earthly Paradise*). Thence they rise, also by virtue of
Divine Care, to the gradual liberation (*the ascent through
the " seven realms of Cato "*) of their "elective judgment "
or *will* from the seven evil habits (*the seven wounds, the*

[1] *Parad.* xxi, 26–27.

[2] This is the anagogic sense of the biblical symbol, which right
reason (*Vergil*) presents to man's imagination (*Dante*), of his moral state
through the ages (*Old Man of Crete,* see above, page 70), beginning
with the age of Saturn, under whom "the world of old was chaste."
The great old man turns his back on Damietta, that is, on Egypt, the
earliest seat of human monarchy, and looks to Rome, the predestined
new seat of that universal monarchy which is to assure to human kind
the felicity of this life.   [3] Cf. *De monarchia,* treatise i, chap. 16.

[4] Such a "conversion" is symbolized by the passage of Dante,
guided by Vergil, from our hemisphere to that one which was chosen
"for human nature as its nest."

seven P's), which are generated in us by the disposition to evil which is consequent on the *vulneratio naturae*.

Thus the grace of God restores to man the faculty of returning to that state of righteousness from which he had voluntarily departed. Thus, in the midst of a world "perfectly disposed," and obedient to "the voice of one sole prince of the Roman people,"[1] there may triumph the bringer of beatitude of the human race, brought to earth by the Word through the Church of Rome (*the triumphal car*) ; that is, the Christian Faith, the Supernatural Truth revealed to man by the Holy Spirit in the way that we already know. And through this, mankind has also the means whereby it may be restored to eternal beatitude,[2] since it is free to devote itself to that "activity of its own virtue," in which earthly happiness consists, in consonance with the habit of good election (Matilda) consequent on the regained freedom of elective judgment. And when its intellect has wings to follow the blissful demonstrations of the bringer of beatitude, it can also in life enjoy a foretaste of this beatitude (as does Dante's soul, according to the allegorical "truth" of the poem).

2. The hidden "doctrine" and the ultimate end of the threefold action (imaginary, allegorical, anagogic). Such is the supersense of the allegory of the poem. From the double "truth" hidden under the "veil," that is, from the "story of Dante's wandering and of his spiritual regeneration," and from the "story of the wandering and of the regeneration of mankind," unfolds that "doctrine" that the reader ought to extract from the work for his own instruction. And this too is double : the *moral* which

---

[1] *Conv.* treatise iv, chap. 5.

[2] Before the coming of the bringer of beatitude to man, "human spirits were not saved" (*Inf.* iv, 63).

proceeds from the allegorical sense, and the *political* which
is drawn from the anagogic. Once the allegory is discovered, every one who goes "intently noting" for his own
use the moral sense in literary compositions can infer from
them to what supreme ends he ought to aspire, and what
means he has at his disposal to attain them. Once the
anagoge is discovered, he will be led to seek the cause why
"no one, or few" [1] arrive at the port of salvation, notwithstanding the Redemption effected by Jesus Christ.

Now, if that extraordinary grace which God granted to
Dante was at one time granted to all mankind, how does
it come that men are damned in such great numbers?
How does it come that incontinence (*the she-wolf*) forbids
their progress along the true way, so that they can never-
more reach that gate of the kingdom of the heavens that

> the evil love of souls disuses,
> because it makes the crooked ways seem straight? [2]

The reply is contained in a special allegorical figure,
which Beatrice, that is, Revealed Truth itself, on the
summit of the holy mountain solemnly enjoins the poet
to describe "for profit of the world which lives ill." [3]

In what condition on earth had the Man-God left his
great gift, that is, the Christian religion, when He returned
to heaven with the prophets, the hagiographers, and the
disciples?

She [*Beatrice*] was sitting alone upon the [truthful] ground, like
a guard left there of the chariot which I had seen bound by the bi-
form animal. In a circle the seven Nymphs were making of themselves an enclosure for her, with those lights in their hands which
are secure from Aquilo and from Auster. [4]

---

[1] "Vel nulli, vel pauci, et hi cum difficultate nimia" (*De monarchia*,
the close as cited above).

[2] *Purg.* x, 2–3.   [3] *Purg.* xxxii, 103.   [4] *Purg.* xxxii, 94–99.

So, then, the Supernatural Truth, which the kindness of God has revealed to man, seated in the world which is disposed to good (*the [truthful] ground*), guards the Church of Rome which Christ has bound to the knowledge of good and evil renewed according to the divine rule (*the lofty plant completely "renewed"*); that is to say, to the "new moral law," to the "Christian morality." And round about, as if to protect it, are the seven virtues, theological and cardinal, illuminating all by means of the seven gifts of the Holy Spirit. This great gift is a pure emanation from God, as we have seen — from God in His three forms. For Supernatural Revealed Truth is the reflection of the True Light, of the Supreme Wisdom (*the Word*); the new moral law, whose origin partakes of this Truth,[1] and the Virtues, who guard them both, have their source in the Primal Power, the Divine Power (*the Father*); the lights that these Virtues hold aloft proceed from the Primal Love (*the Holy Spirit*).

The allegorical symbol that Revealed Truth soon after enjoins its faithful follower to describe for the admonition of mortals, represents the evil government which the *donum Dei* has suffered from the moment when Jesus Christ, ascending to heaven, has left it in the world, until the moment in which begins the poet's "fated going" through the three realms of the otherworld.

The triumphal car, after the eagle has left its body "feathered from himself," and after the dragon who has issued from underground has broken the floor, and the feathers have entirely covered it, has become a

[1] The Supernatural Revealed Truth, seated in the shade of the new moral precepts, guards their root, which is her own possession (" Behold her [*Beatrice*] under the new leafage, sitting upon its root "; *Purg.* xxxii, 86–87).

monstrosity; and upon it sin a *fuja*, or "thief," and a giant.
That is to say, that the Church is being impaired in its
natural authority (*the floor*)[1] by the deceit of the devil (*the
dragon*)[2] as soon as the Imperial Power (*the eagle*) made
the famous donation[3] (*the feathers on the body of the car*).
And after it has been entirely covered with worldly goods
(*the other feathers*), it has become monstrously corrupt,
whereby two authorities have become intermingled in an
infamous fashion : the spiritual, legitimate, but which has
become simoniac, whereby it prostitutes the things of God
for gold and silver, and the temporal, illegitimate, and
usurping. The first is appropriately represented by the
thief, the brazen harlot, seated

> secure as a fortress on a high mountain

on the car which has become a monstrosity. The second
finds its full and perfect poetic representation in the giant:
the "son of the earth"[4] in rebellion against the "Supreme Jove . . . crucified for us," and who has come to
nullify the work of the Latter by planting himself erect, by
the side of the seated *fuja* (thief), on the "holy structure"

[1] The floor of the car, on which Revealed Truth triumphed in the
world *optime disposito*, that is, of the "vessel" (*Purg.* xxxiii, 34) destined
to receive and spread abroad among the peoples the *documenta* of the
knowledge which has its roots in this Truth, represents the authority
whereby the Church obtains faith and obedience among men and thus
imparts to them the *rivelata* (cf. *De monarchia*, iii, 15; *Conv.* iv, 6).
Satan has the satisfaction of being able fraudulently to appropriate a
part of it to himself, thus again obtaining credit among men (" he drew
out part of the floor, and went [swaggering] away "). [*Purg.* xxxii, 135.]

[2] The dragon represents diabolic fraud, as does Geryon the human,
and the two symbols correspond to each other. For the wild beast with
the pointed tail has of our nature only "the face of a just man"; all
the rest is " of a serpent," that is, of a diabolic nature, exactly like that
of the dragon who fixes his malignant tail in the floor of the car, and
shatters it.   [3] [The so-called False donation of Constantine.]

[4] Cf. *Inf.* xxxi, 121.

which has wrongly become the receptacle of worldly things, and so is impaired by deceit of the devil. The emissary of hell, the emissary of that emperor of the woeful realm who is by far the most monstrous among the giants,[1] is quite naturally a giant:

> for where the faculty of the mind
> is added to evil will and to power,
> the human race can make no defense against it.[2]

This giant, master of the car by usurpation, looses it from the tree to which the griffon has attached it, and drags it away through the wood. That is to say, that the Church, enslaved to the temporal authority of the Pope, can no longer attend to its ministry as a dispenser of the restored *knowledge of good and evil* in conformity with the divine wishes, that is, of the moral Christian law. That is why

> the shepherd who is in advance [*the Pope*]
> can chew the cud, but has not his hoofs divided:

that is, he can meditate and know the holy texts, but no longer possesses the discernment of good and evil, well symbolized by the cleft hoof.[3] And that is why, consequently,

> the people, who see their guide aim only
> at that good for which they are greedy,
> feed upon that, and seek no further.

Whereby, notwithstanding the work of Redemption, *incontinence* (that is, that infirmity of the soul through which man is unsuccessful in controlling his appetites) having come into the world with original sin, and having

---

[1] Cf. *Inf.* xxxiv, 28–33.   [2] *Inf.* xxxi, 55–57.
[3] *Purg.* xvi, 98–99. This is the *fissio ungulae* of St. Thomas (*Summa theologica*, I 2ae, quest. 102, art. 6, ad 1um).

been later rendered harmless to men of good will by the
Son of God by means of the great gift (the Christian religion) ; from the time that the latter was weakened by the
serpent, *incontinence* reasserted its deadly former rule, and

> lets not anyone pass along her way,
> but so hinders him that she kills him.

Dante, by a most unusual favor of God, has been liber-
ated from the "beast without peace" by means of *right
reason in the fullness of time* and *revealed supernatural
truth*. This favor was once granted to all men ! Wherefor
the Emperor was ordained by God to redirect or to keep
in the straight way that reason which is to lead us to
temporal happiness by means of the teachings of philosophy ; and the Pope was ordained by God to lead men in
the straight way by means of the teachings of religion.
The mingling of these two rules, which had become corrupt, in the Church of Rome (*the sinning of the thief
with the giant on the car*) is the cause of all the evil :

> Say thou henceforth, that the Church of Rome,
> through confounding in itself two modes of rule,
> falls in the mire, and defiles itself and its burden.[1]

To point out such a condition, to prophesy the necessary
remedy, such is the ultimate end of the threefold action
of the poem, *imaginary*, *allegorical*, and *anagogic*.

Then who will be the hound by whom the "old she-
wolf," symbolizing incontinence, will be

> put back again in Hell
> there whence envy first sent her forth ? [2]

Or, leaving aside the imagery, who will be the one who,
disdaining money and property, will drive out incontinence,

---

[1] *Purg.* xvi, 127–129.   [2] *Inf.* i, 110–111; *Purg.* xx, 10–15.

which the devil, envious of the felicity of the first man, introduced into the world by original sin ?

He will be no other than a minister or vicar of that "messenger from God," of that *dux* (DXV, "five hundred ten and five"), in a word that one among the two guides of men (the *two Suns*) who is now lacking, and who is necessary. The leader, that is, the Emperor

shall slay the thief together with that giant who is sinning with her,[1]

thus taking away the monstrous excrescence, originating from the devil, upon the gift of God as it was bestowed upon mortals :

> The eagle that left its feathers on the car,
> whereby it became a monster, and then a prey,
> shall not be for all time without an heir.

Its minister or vicar, in great likelihood Cangrande della Scala,[2] will see to it that continence is restored to that position (*the low Italy*) where the unbridled wills of ecclesiastics now rule in temporal domination, and thus he will be able to oust the beast without peace from every

---

[1] *Purg.* xxxiii, 42–45.

[2] "And its nation will be between Feltro and Feltro" (*Inf.* i, 105) that is, between Feltro and Montefeltro, the designation (of a kind not uncommon in Dante) of upper Italy. Taking it thus (and this explanation is as obvious as the others are strained), we must exclude the idea that the hound is the emperor himself, who is, certainly, not an Italian. Besides, according to the political ideas of Alighieri clearly expressed in the *De monarchia*, purging the world of incontinence by restraining human cupidity is the office of the secular leader ; whence it is natural to think that the hound may symbolize the minister chosen by him to give chase to the wolf. Cangrande was the imperial vicar, he was of upper Italy, he was the one not caring "for silver" (*Parad.* xvii, 84), and fit for "incredible things." It is a most reasonable hypothesis that, when "some sparkles of his virtue" appeared, Dante should insert in the prologue of the work, whose final cantica we know to have been dedicated to Cangrande, that prophecy which expressed a hope of his, or at least an invocation.

place. Then " the vessel that the serpent broke," that is, the Church, will return whole and pure. Then, the confusion between the two powers having been removed, mankind, guided by the Emperor to temporal felicity according to philosophic teachings, will again acquire the right use of reason, and will be no longer hindered in the way to Good by incontinence ; and, guided by the Pope to the beatitude of eternal life according to spiritual teachings, it will be able to enjoy the bliss of the contemplation of the True.

Thus, thanks to the two rules that are " the remedy against the infirmity of sin," [1] its affection, which finds its satisfaction in Good, and its intellect, which finds its satisfaction in Truth, will be no longer infirm, as now, but both will be sane and free in the tranquillity of peace.[2]

3. The manifest " doctrine": the sciences of the Trivium. Having thus examined the lofty doctrine, ethical and political, which is hidden under the veil of the most stupendous imagery that a poet's mind has ever conceived, we must now give a rapid glance over the far more varied doctrine that the letter of the *Commedia* encloses. I have said more varied, for, by the side of purely philosophical digressions, such as (only to cite the longest and most important) those put into Vergil's mouth, on fortune (*Inf.* vii, 70 et seq.), on the various forms of moral evil (*Inf.* xi, 22 et seq.), on love and its disorderly states (*Purg.* xvii, 91 et seq. and xviii, 19 et seq.), by the side of purely political digressions, such as that put into the mouth of Marco Lombardi on the reason for the " bad

---

[1] " Sunt ergo hujusmodi regimina remedia contra infirmitatem peccati" (*De monarchia*, treatise iii, chap. 4).

[2] Cf. *De monarchia*, treatise i, last chap., and treatise iii, last chap.

conduct" of men (*Purg*. xvi, 64 et seq.), or that other put
into the mouth of Beatrice on the "present life of wretched
mortals" (*Parad*. xxvii, 121 et seq.), in the course of the
third cantica there are a great number of theological digressions — often very extended and subtile. There are
also some which have to do with the loftiest natural truths,
implied in or posited by supernatural truths, like that of
Statius on the origin of man and the creation of the soul
(*Purg*. xxv, 34 et seq.).

Furthermore, all seven "sciences of the Trivium and
Quadrivium" (*grammar, dialectics*, and *rhetoric; arithmetic, music, geometry*, and *astronomy*) have had their
part in the composition of the poem ; the last of these
also offers material for digressions. What a lofty concept
of these sciences Dante had, appears from the *Convivio*,
where he demonstrates subtly and at length their respective resemblances to each of the seven heavens of the
planets.[1]

In the *Commedia* we see grammar studiously observed
in those rules which, while intended exclusively for Latin,
Alighieri has applied in such a masterly manner to the
common idiom. It is clear that he has not contented himself with the indiscriminate use of the Florentine dialect in
his poem, but has availed himself of his maternal speech
with true grammatical knowledge, after having studied it
patiently and lovingly. To this study he was induced by
the admiration which he felt for "the smoothness of its
syllables, the propriety of its rules, and the sweet discourses
that are made of it,"[2] and stimulated by the noble desire
to be of service to princes and barons, gentlemen and ladies,
who were all ignorant of Latin, by offering them a work

[1] Treatise ii, chap. 14.   [2] *Conv.* treatise i, chap. 10.

which they could understand and from which they could obtain both pleasure and profit.[1]

And dialectics has a considerable part in the Dantesque poem, as well as grammatical science. That argumentation, according to the principles of logic laid down by the Schoolmen, of which Alighieri makes use as he "proves and disproves" (we should say, exposes and refutes) through the mouth of his personages, especially in the third cantica, — that argumentation, according to the ideas of the poet teacher, ought certainly to aim at giving practical instruction in the science that *vera docet*. The determination of the dialectic methods used by Dante in the course of his work, where he means to banish darkness from the intellect in order better to "make clear" the truth, is as yet a closed book to the curiosity of Dantologists.

And the same is true as regards rhetoric. The artifices and turns of thought which conform to the precepts of Quintilian or to the arts of "poetical composition"[2] have only lately attracted the attention of students. It has been observed that the rhetorical artifice called *anaphora* appears in the fifth canto of the *Inferno*, where three successive terzine begin with the word "love"; as well as in the fourth canto, where the proximity of the words *honorable*, *honorest*, *honorableness*, *honored*, *honor* [verb], *honor* [noun] (verses 70–133) is certainly not fortuitous. *Plays on words* ("turned many turns," "I think that he thought that I thought," etc.) occur not infrequently in the poem,

---

[1] One may read in the introductory treatise of the *Convivio* the very charming pages in which Dante exposes the reasons which have induced him to prefer the common idiom to Latin. The continual change in living languages is keenly noted, as well as obsolete words, neologisms, or words whose form has varied in the space of not more than half a century.　　　　　　[2] ["trovare."]

as well as *alliterations, assonances, internal rhymes,* and the like. In the twelfth canto of the *Purgatorio* four terzine begin with the word *vedea*,[1] four others with *O*, four others with *mostrava*,[2] all consecutive. The threefold series is closed by a terzina in which each verse begins with one of the words just mentioned, and in the same order; so that, taking the initials, we have the acrostic VOM (and, with the *o* of *mostrava*, VOMO). Nor is this artifice purely a matter of form; it reflects a logical coördination of thought, since three classes of punished pride correspond to three series of terzine, which are all brought together in the last example (that of the city of Troy), which in itself forms an epitome of those preceding. And this is done in such a way that in the terzina which contains this last example are summed up the forms which serve to distinguish the others, and whose initials designate *man* [*uomo*] as a proud being, by *antonomasia*. And, as here the sins of man's pride, so in the nineteenth canto of the *Paradiso* the sins of the rulers of mankind are denounced in three terzine that begin *Lì si vedrà*,[3] in three more that begin *Vedrassi*,[4] and in three more that begin with *E*.[5] From this we obtain, by uniting the initials of the three series, the acrostic LVE, to admonish us that in the things enumerated in these terzine is the *lue*, " the contagion," that corrupts the administration of justice among Christians.

4. **The sciences of the Quadrivium : the astronomical details and the data of the Dantesque journey.** All this proves that Dante had the same respect for the art of rhetoric that his age lavished upon it. Nor in his poem

---

[1] [I saw.]   [2] [It showed.]   [3] [There shall be seen.]
[4] [Shall be seen.]   [5] [And.]

does he show himself less devoted to music, the first among the sciences of the Quadrivium. Alighieri shows clearly in the episode of Casella,[1] the extraordinary power that music has over the mind. In this he pictures that the spirits, which are longing to run and "strip off the slough" that forbids them the beatific vision, delay to listen to the melodies of the celebrated Florentine singer, as though not caring for anything else. And of these are Vergil, who impersonates right reason, and Dante himself, who nevertheless is eagerly desirous of beginning the work of his own moral regeneration. Furthermore, the *musical quality* of the diction in the *Commedia* is marvelous. There abound in it references to sound (especially in relation with light), to natural acoustic phenomena, to the song of birds, to musical instruments, to song, unisonal, polyphonic, monodic, and lastly to the harmony of the spheres, which is alone capable of giving us a superhuman idea of beauty. In a word, Dante has, in his encyclopedic poem, indirectly given us valuable ideas on the science of sounds, which has also contributed to the greatness of his art.[2]

To the men of the Middle Ages music, considered as a science, seemed inseparable from arithmetic; they recognized, as did Pythagoras, that its essence was in numbers. And numbers, in the Dantesque poem, give a norm and control to the artist's imagination. For we know that 1, 3, 9, and 10 are considered as the basis of its division into the three realms of the otherworld and of their inhabitants, of the ordering of the universe, and of its motor intelligences.

[1] *Purg.* ii, 106–123.
[2] On this point (as well as on the musical compositions inspired by the *Commedia*) see the fine book of A. Bonaventura, *Dante e la musica*, Leghorn, Giusti, 1904.

And line is treated as number : Inferno, Purgatorio, and Paradiso are constructed according to the fundamental conceptions of geometry, as it appears even in the plans which we have drawn, which are purely geometrical. But it would be idle, in our estimation, and harmful to the æsthetic side of the work, arbitrarily to usurp the place of the author and, by making his purely imaginary edifice subject to natural laws (for instance, that of gravity) to fix exactly measures and distances which he himself did not care to indicate, lest he do violence to the imagination and to art itself.

And it seems to us that we should think of the astronomical data in the same way. Dante conceives his journey to the otherworld as having lasted seven days, from the "beginning of the morning" of Good Friday, the eighth of April, to the afternoon of the Thursday after Easter, the fourteenth of April, of the year 1300 (the year of Jubilee).[1] Only in a general way could Dante have been

[1] Very valid arguments support this date of 1300. (1) If Dante was born (as seems certain) in 1265, in this very year, that is in 1300, he would have us believe that he issued forth from the dark wood ("midway upon the journey of our life"), since in the *Convivio* (treatise iv, chap. 23) he compares the life of man to an arch, the keystone of which is the thirty-fifth year. (2) Guido Cavalcanti was alive when Dante visited the lost peoples. This imaginary visit is then anterior to the twenty-eighth of August, 1300, for Cavalcanti died on that day. (3) Casella says in the second canto of the *Purg.* verses 98–99, that the angel by whom the good souls are received at the mouth of the Tiber "for three months has taken with all peace whoso has wished to enter"; and the indulgence of the Jubilee began about three months before Easter, 1300. (4) Cangrande della Scala, born the ninth of March, 1291, was "only nine years" old (*Parad.* xvii, 80) when Dante undertook his imaginary journey. We are, then, in 1300. (5) Beatrice died the eighth of June, 1290. In April of 1300 Dante was without sight of her for almost ten years. This agrees with the "ten years' thirst" of which he speaks in the *Purg.* xxxii, 2. (6) 1300 is the "hundredth" year of the thirteenth century. And Folco of Marseilles says in the *Parad.* ix, 40: "This hundredth year shall yet come round five times." (7) Corrado

able or have wished to make the time references, which nevertheless he does not fail to insert here and there in his imaginary story, correspond exactly to the real position of the sun, moon, or stars in the year and month in which he is pleased to suppose that his "fated going" took place. It may be that, writing after the lapse of several years, he could not remember exactly how things had gone in 1300, or that he never could have imagined that one of these days astronomers by profession would pry into them with all the perfected means for such critical examination, just as if he had not told a story, but rather an actual happening, which must be demonstrated to be in conformity with the facts—even in the least detail! Hence the inexactness in astronomical detail which has made, and makes, many excellent men wrongly reject the date of 1300 as that of the Dantesque journey, substituting therefor 1301 in order to clear Dante from the reproach of being an inaccurate astronomer. A baseless reproach, for it was sufficient for his ends to convey some general ideas of the science, independent of their mathematical correspondence to the date of the imaginary action.

And such general ideas abound in the poem. So much so, that for the modern reader many passages in the *Commedia* that contain them have great need of comment; and more than one, like the famous one on the "concubine of old Tithonus," [1] or that other on the point of meeting

Malaspina says to the poet that seven years will not pass before the latter will have personal experience of the worth of his "honored race" (*Purg.* viii, 133-139). And if we may consider these words to have been said in April, 1300, this prophecy *a posteriori* is exact; for Dante was a guest of the Malaspina in 1306. (8) Ciacco predicts to Dante the sanguinary struggle between the partisans of the Donati and Cerchi the first of May, 1300. So then the poet's visit to the damned is conceived of as being anterior to that day.   [1] *Purg.* ix, 1 et seq.

" which joins four circles with three crosses,"[1] have given and still give occasion for much controversy. In this respect, too, Dante's poem must have been profitable reading for his contemporaries; and also as regards instruction of a geographical as well as astronomical nature. Geographico-astronomical is, for example, that short *excursus* with which Folco of Marseilles judges it opportune to preface his explanation of his own state of being, which he gives the poet at the latter's request:

> The greatest valley in which the water spreads
> — began then his words —
> [forth from] that sea which garlands the earth,
> extends between its discordant shores so far
> counter to the sun, that it makes a meridian
> where first it is wont to make the horizon.[2]

In these verses, not easy to understand at the first glance, Dante desires to teach by mouth of Folco that the element *earth* is furrowed by a great hollow, in which spreads the element *water*, which surrounds it; that, since the upper terrestrial hemisphere has Jerusalem for its center, this hollow (the Mediterranean) stretches from the west to the east through a full ninety degrees, between shores that do not correspond mutually in their horizontal conformation, so that it has at one of its extremities as meridian the very circle that the other has for its horizon.

If we add to these cosmographic ideas those of descriptive geography which are met with at every step in the course of the work, especially in the comparisons,— if we take into consideration the stupendous pictures of mountain peaks,[3] of river courses,[4] of the swelling of the latter

---

[1] *Parad*. i, 38–39.   [2] *Parad*. ix, 82–87.
[3] *Parad*. xxi, 106 et seq.
[4] *Inf*. xx, 61 et seq., and *Purg*. xiv, 16 et seq.

by rains,[1] of the falling of water in the form of a cascade,[2] of its freezing on the slope of the mountain,[3] of the land-slide caused by the slip of masses of earth,[4] all these and others always accompanied with the precise designation of places, or location of countries, or determination of terri-torial boundaries,[5] — we shall assign also to geographical science a considerable part in that encyclopedic learning with which Alighieri's poem abounds in the letter.

5. **How the doctrinal elements are blended with the artistic in the *Commedia*.** Such a copious doctrinal con-tent, both manifest and hidden, does not do violence to art in the *Commedia*. On the contrary, it enhances it, inasmuch as it offers to the poet's imagination, as well as to his intellect, a thousand opportunities of testing the limit of its power. And Dante's ability in putting into verse things which are difficult to think upon is surely one of his greatest titles to glory. Science and poetry, as was the aim of the men of the Middle Ages,[6] are interwoven in a masterly manner in the *Commedia*, and illumine each other. The lady of his love and the author of his predi-lection, Beatrice and Vergil, live again in it in the glory of their symbolism, which in its turn, having lost its abstract quality, palpitates with real life. For, in the measure that Dante has been able to draw and color his imaginary otherworld so as to give it life, so has he suc-ceeded in giving a plastic relief and almost statuesque majesty to his abstractions.

---

[1] *Purg.* v, 115 et seq.   [2] *Inf.* xvi, 94 et seq.   [3] *Purg.* xxx, 85 et seq.
[4] *Inf.* xii, 4 et seq.
[5] It should be observed how exactly the boundaries of the Kingdom of Naples are stated in the eighth canto of the *Paradiso* (61–63) and those of the March of Treviso in the ninth (25–27).
[6] See above, pp. 21–22.

And neither can one say that the ultramundane part of his marvelous poem, the scientific and theological, has in any way done injury to the human, the psychological, and the political. It is not merely with their symbolism and allegory, nor with their scholasticism alone, that the Middle Ages are again revealed to our eyes, but with their habits, their institutions, and all the affections and feelings proper to them. So that Empire and Papacy, Communes and Lords, Courtiers and Ecclesiastics, are there associated in a faithful and complete historical picture of that age. And from the satire and invective, both frequent, issues an admirably lifelike representation of the civil and political conditions of Florence, of Italy, of Christianity. The episode of the Florentine Ciacco, who describes the corruption of the "divided city" and predicts its misfortunes; that of Filippo Argenti, whom those immersed in the mud of the Styx rend as if to satisfy the author's private vengeance; that of Farinata degli Uberti, magnanimous and fearless even in his burning tomb; that of Brunetto, who vituperates his native Florence with low abuse; and those of Guido da Montefeltro, of Sordello, of Forese Donati, of Cacciaguida, etc., are miracles of painting no less than of poetry, "among which (we may say with Isidoro del Lungo) the old Commune with its memories, the Florentine family, and the Italian city, the glories, the faults, the misfortunes of the nation, live again before our eyes." Even when, as in the *Paradiso*, the poet surrounds the historical personages that he puts upon the scene with a radiance which the eye cannot endure, they rise before us there full of life, so that we seem to see them. In narrations such as that of Count Ugolino, or that of the love and death of Francesca da Rimini, neither can the eye

of a critic (as Foscolo justly observes) ever perceive all
the art, nor can the imagination of a poet equal it, nor
can a soul, however cold, not feel it. Never has poetic
imagery presented itself to an artist's mind with so much
clearness of outline and so much color of truth. With the
word quickened by the image, Dante paints and sculptures.

And so, having penetrated the hidden senses of the
Commedia, having pointed out the encyclopedic variety of
instruction which it encloses, there would remain for us
(the more pleasing in that it is not less arduous) the study
of the secrets of the art by which Alighieri in his masterpiece has so skillfully blended the most diverse elements
with a peculiar clearness of expression, even in the most
abstruse concepts and in those facts not easily expressed ;
with a language which assists the idea, and fixes, as it
were on the wing, the image which starts forth from the
subtly observed truth ; with a poetic technique so infinitely
varied and profound as to offer in itself alone matter for a
complete treatise.[1] There would remain for us to see in
this poem, in which is summarized all the knowledge of
the Italian laymen tenaciously perpetuated in the Middle
Ages, the manner in which our supreme artist has coupled
the grotesque and the sublime, the observation of nature,
and the contemplation of the lofty truths of faith.

But this is beside our purpose, nor could it be contained
in the limits of a modest handbook.

[1] See the fine study of E. G. Parodi on *La rima e i vocaboli in rima
nella D. C.* (in the *Bullettino della società dantesca italiana*, vol. iii).

CHAPTER VI

FAME AND FORTUNE OF THE *COMMEDIA*

1. Composition and publication of the work. 2. Commentaries upon the *Commedia* written in the fourteenth century. 3. Commentaries written in succeeding centuries. 4. Fame and imitations of the poem from the fourteenth to the sixteenth century. 5. Fame of the poem in the seventeenth and eighteenth centuries. 6. The cult of Dante and the state of the studies on the *Commedia* in our times.

1. The composition and publication of the work. We know very little of the manner in which Dante composed the *Commedia*. When did he begin it? Probably not long after his going into exile. How did he carry forward his work? Certainly slowly and with exertion, for the poem " made him lean for many years." [1] We have no proof that he ever showed any portions to his friends, or that his children were well informed of his intentions.

The *Inferno* and *Purgatorio*, which could not have been completed in their present form before 1314,[2] were published about 1318. This is evident from the Latin eclogues which Dante himself and Giovanni del Virgilio exchanged at about that date. For the latter, in referring to Lethe and Statius, gives us to understand that he is acquainted with the whole second cantica ; and Alighieri says in the first eclogue that when the whirling spheres and the

---

[1] *Parad.* xxv, 3.

[2] From verses 79–81 of the nineteenth canto of the *Inferno* it appears that when Dante wrote them the death of Pope Clement V (April 20, 1314) had already occurred. The ninety-sixth verse of the seventh canto of the *Purgatorio* alludes to the unfortunate result of the enterprise of Henry VII in Italy (1313).

blessed " shall stand revealed " (*patebunt*), as the *infera regna* are already, then his joy will be to bind his brow with laurel and with ivy.

He expected much from the publication of the third cantica, which had a loftier subject than the others ; as a proof of which we have the famous beginning of its twenty-fifth canto : " If it ever happen that the sacred poem," etc. He wished its publication entrusted to Cangrande della Scala, and he must have sent him a copy of it to that end. But it appears that Verona's lord did not hasten its publication, and in the meantime the poet died. A rhymester friend of Dante, Giovanni Quirini of Venice, who probably expressed to him his own impatience, and had learned from him that the work was in the hands of Cangrande and that Dante wished it given to the world by the same hand, addressed a prayer to the Scaliger in the form of a sonnet, of which this is the second part :

[I am your very faithful servitor
   Who gladly would the sacred glory see
   Of Paradise whereof the poet sings :
Therefore I pray you that of such a plant
   It please you to show forth the beauteous flowers ;
   For they bear fruit worthy their fabricant.
Who did intend (and still intends, I know)
   That by you first throughout the world be spread
   To other men this so great work of his.]

Verses that we believe to have been written during the lifetime of Alighieri, as indeed every one interprets them at first sight. The phrase " for they bear fruit worthy their fabricant " should be taken, " for they bear fruit befitting their maker." Accordingly the good Quirini says to Cangrande : " I pray you to publish this work ; not alone because of its beauty (*the fair flowers*), but because of its great fruitfulness. Thus every one will be able to ' gather fruit from his reading.' " [1]

2. Commentaries on the *Commedia* written in the fourteenth century.

That a work like the *Commedia*, so varied in content, so copious in doctrine, so profound in its meanings, so lofty in its aims, should have had, as soon as it was given to the world, interpreters desirous of aiding us to a full and correct understanding of it, cannot surprise us. The poet's sons, Jacopo and Pietro, under-took such a work, albeit with widely differing qualifications. Passing over the question, brought forward anew, of an older Latin commentary of the poem,[2] Jacopo Alighieri in his *Chiose* [Glosses],[3] written between 1322 and 1324, has tried in an elementary fashion to reveal the allegorical senses of the *Inferno*, exercising a considerable influence over the commentators who followed him. Much more scholarly and learned in philosophic and theological dis-cipline, his brother Pietro, in his commentary to the whole *Commedia*, composed in Latin between 1340 and 1341, also proposed to explain the allegoric and doctrinal part of the poem in particular, but in accordance with the church fathers, the philosophers, and the Latin classics.[4]

---

[1] *Inf.* xx, 19–20.

[2] See F. P. Luiso, *Di un commento ined. alla Div. Comm. fonte dei più antichi commentatori*, Firenze, 1903, and *Tra chiose e commenti antichi alla Div. Comm.*, in the *Arch. stor. ital.*, part i, 1893, and part i, 1904 (but cf. M. Barbi, in the *Bull. della società dantesca ital.*, *N. S.*, Nos. 194–229). Professor Luiso has published only the second volume of this commentary, referring to the *Purgatorio* (*Chiose di Dante le quali fece el figliuolo co le sue mani*, Firenze, 1904).

[3] *Chiose alla cantica dell' Inf. di D. A. attribuite a Jacopo suo figlio*, ecc. [Glosses to the Cantica of the Inferno of Dante Alighieri, attrib-uted to Jacopo his Son, etc.], Florence, 1848.

[4] *Petri Allegherii super Dantis ipsius genitoris Comoediam Commen-tarium*, etc., Florence, 1845. Pietro di Dante, having compiled this Commentary, later had the idea of recasting it entirely. This second

Similar to that of Jacopo, and of about the same date, are commentaries on the first cantica alone by Ser Graziolo de' Bambaglioli of Bologna, who, unlike Dante's sons, gave his especial attention to the literal sense, using as the basis of his explanation the Bible and the church fathers; [1] by an anonymous writer of scant culture, incoherent in his interpretations of the allegories, inexact even when he alludes to very recent facts; [2] and by Guido da Pisa, whose work is still veiled in the mystery of the unpublished.[3] Jacopo della Lana (another Bolognese) wrote between 1323 and 1328, perhaps in 1327, a full commentary to the whole poem, much more read than the preceding, in fact the best known of all the early commentaries,[4] perhaps by reason of the considerable Aristotelic and scholastic learning, of the frequent learned digressions, and, above all, of the narrative part which abounds in it. For us modern students it has less value, either because Della Lana shows that he knows the classics

redaction is preserved in a codex at the Vatican. Afterwards, not yet content, he retouched his revision so as to make a third redaction, which we have in a codex Ashburnham of the Laurentian Library of Florence.

[1] *Il commento più antico e la più antica versione dell' Inferno dal codice di Sandaniele del Friuli*, Udine, 1892. An early Italian version of this Latin commentary appeared anonymously in Florence in 1848.

[2] *Chiose anon. alla prima cantica della D. C.*, ecc., Turin, 1865. (These are the Glosses called " of Selmi," from the name of their first editor; they were reprinted, according to the codex Marciano, in the *Collezione di opuscoli danteschi*, Nos. 61–62, Città di Castello, 1900.)

[3] This is preserved in manuscript in the library of the Duc d'Aumale at Chantilly, and in the British Museum (partially also in other codices, as in the Laurenziano xl, 2). An " Explanation " of the poem in *terza rima* by the same author, with an accompanying Latin commentary, was published in the *Propugnatore* of 1888.

[4] This is the one which accompanies the *Commedia* in the editions of Venice, 1477, and Milan, 1478, and was several times translated into Latin during the fourteenth century. It has been recently reprinted in the *Collezione di opere inedite o rare* (Bologna, 1866–1867).

only indirectly for the most part, or because he does not understand the meaning of many words,[1] or, finally, because he distorts the history of his own times, or because he betrays an artlessness regarding ancient history that appears incredible.[2] More trustworthy, although not so early, is the *Ottimo commento* (1334 *ca.*), the work of a Florentine (perhaps Ser Andrea Lancia, a well-known translator and adapter) who says that he knew Dante personally.[3] It is an exposition of the entire poem, based without much order on previous commentaries, which the author often copies, though quoting and often discussing and availing himself of the opinions of others. This commentator knows Vergil and other classics directly, he understands and writes well the language of his glorious fellow citizen, he is the first to put to profit the *Convivio* and to explain Dante by Dante, and he appears generally well informed on the history of his times.

These are the commentaries which have come down to us, and which, since they were written in the twenty years following the poet's death, are of venerable antiquity and contain explanations which have passed from one to another of the subsequent commentaries. Later, but still of the fourteenth century (and hence very authoritative)

[1] "*Accento* [accent] means almost 'bellowed'" (I, 129). "*Ruscello* [streamlet] means 'bloody'" (I, 179). "*Macigno* [rock] in the Florentine tongue means '*stancaruolo*,' that is, deceit and subtile caution in working another's harm" (I, 179).

[2] Mucius Scævola, who kills Julius Cæsar (III, 68), and Scipio Africanus, who becomes emperor of Rome with Augustus, both enter Rome in triumph on one of those cars, on which "when the troops of the commune took the field the rectors went, and a priest went on it with all the church paraphernalia and sung mass on the aforesaid car" (II, 356).

[3] *L'ottimo commento della D. C., testo ined. d'un contemporaneo di Dante*, ecc. [The Best Commentary on the Divine Comedy, an Unpublished Text of a Contemporary of Dante, etc.], Pisa, 1827–1829.

are the Commentary in Latin to the whole *Commedia* by Benvenuto dei Rambaldi da Imola[1]; those in Italian, very extensive, by Francesco da Buti[2] and by an Anonymous Florentine[3]; and, above all, the exposition of the first sixteen cantos of the *Inferno* (and a few lines of the seventeenth), made with learning and with loving care, by a writer who is at last worthy of the poet commented upon — Giovanni Boccaccio.[4] He, charged by the Signoria of Florence, read in public the *Commedia* in the church of Santo Stefano di Badia, from the twenty-third of October, 1373, for sixty consecutive days (excluding festivals), as long as his health lasted.

3. Commentaries on the *Commedia* from the fifteenth to the nineteenth century. Even in the century of Humanism the poem had interpreters whom we may not pass over in silence : the Franciscan, Giovanni Bertoldi da Serravalle di Rimini, bishop of Fermo, who in 1416 translated into Latin and commented upon the *Commedia* (following Benvenuto da Imola, his master) for his colleagues assembled with him at the Council of Constance;[5]

---

[1] *Benvenuti de Rambaldis de Imola Comentum super Dantis Aldigherij Comoediam*, etc., Florence, 1887.

[2] *Commento di Francesco da Buti sopra la Div. Comedia* [Commentary of Francesco da Buti on the Divine Comedy], Pisa, 1858–1862.

[3] *Commento alla Div. Com. d'Anonimo Fiorentino del secolo XIV*, ecc. [Commentary on the Divine Comedy by an Anonymous Florentine of the Fourteenth Century, etc.], Bologna, 1866–1874.

[4] *Il Comento di Gio. Boccaccio sopra la Commedia* [The Commentary of Gio. Boccaccio on the Comedy], Florence, 1724 (the best edition is that of Le Monnier, Florence, 1863). Certain *Chiose sopra Dante* [Glosses on Dante] which were published in 1846 at Florence were falsely attributed to Boccaccio (and hence were known under the name of the False Boccaccio).

[5] *Fratris Johannis de Serravalle Ord. Min. Episcopi Firmani translatio et comentum totius libri Dantis Aldigherii cum textu italico Fratris Bartholomaei a Colle ejusdem ordinis*, etc., Prato, 1891.

Guiniforte dei Bargigi, or da Barzizza (one of those humanists who did not neglect Italian literature for Latin and for classical antiquity), who explained the first cantica ;[1] the anonymous author of that commentary to the whole *Commedia*, who goes under the name of Stefano Talice da Ricaldone ;[2] and, much more important, Cristoforo Landino da Pratovecchio, valiant restorer in his own Florence of literary compositions written in Italian, to whom we owe a commentary of the *Commedia*[3] especially devoted to explaining its hidden meanings (according to the philosophy of Plato, instead of that of Aristotle, which, as we know, was the one really followed by Dante), in which he unites the best of the commentaries of Pietro di Dante (for the theological part), of Francesco da Buti (for the allegories), of Boccaccio and of Benvenuto da Imola (for the historical part), adding to these the flower of a copious and varied learning.

This commentary of Landino had, for this reason, great good fortune ; it was reprinted often during the first years which followed its publication,[4] and no one else dared attempt an exposition of the *Commedia* until towards the

[1] *Lo Inferno della Comm. di D. A. col comento di Guiniforto delli Bargigi* [The Inferno of the Comedy of D. A. with the Commentary of Guiniforto delli Bargigi], Marseilles, 1838.

[2] *La Comm. di D. A. col commento ined. di Stefano Talice da Ricaldone* [The Comedy of D. A. with the Unpublished Commentary of Stefano Talice da Ricaldone], 2ª ed., Milan, 1888. Talice was not the author or compiler, but only the amanuensis of this commentary, which is little more than a compendium of Benvenuto (cf. *Biblioteca delle scuole ital.* [Library of the Italian Schools], v, 11 ; and *Gazzetta letteraria* [Literary Gazette], xvii, 2).

[3] *Comento di Cristoforo Landini fiorentino sopra la commedia di D. A.*, ecc. [Commentary of Cristoforo Landini the Florentine on the Comedy of D. A., etc.], Florence, 1481.

[4] From 1481 to the end of the fifteenth century it was reproduced six times, and ten times in the following century.

end of the middle of the sixteenth century. Then Alessandro Vellutello of Lucca, profiting largely by the work of Landino, took up the exegesis of Dante for his own account.[1] And Bernardino Daniello, also of Lucca, with a praiseworthy aim at self-restraint but also with inadequate preparation (especially as concerns the language), again attempted the task, profiting freely by the *Annotazioni su Dante* [Annotations on Dante], as yet unpublished, of his master, Trifon Gabriele.[2] Much more useful to us than these two mediocre commentaries are the "readings" on Dante by Gelli and by Varchi,[3] both well equipped as to language and well acquainted with the philosophy of Aristotle. And we may still consult not without profit the minute and judicious exposition of the first canto of the *Inferno* left us by Pier Francesco Giambullari,[4] and that of the first twenty-nine cantos of the same cantica due to the subtile mind of Lodovico Castelvetro (on account of the many acute observations mingled with unjust censures passed upon the poet).[5]

We must come to the eighteenth century to find new and complete commentaries upon the poem of Dante. In

[1] *La Comedia di D. A. con la nova esposizione di Alessandro Vellutello* [The Comedy of D. A. with the New Exposition of Alessandro Vellutello], Venice, 1544.

[2] *Dante con l'esposizione di Bernardino Daniello da Lucca*, ecc. [Dante with the Exposition of Bernardino Daniello of Lucca, etc.], Venice, 1568.

[3] *Letture edite ed inedite di G. B. Gelli sopra la Commedia di Dante* [Published and unpublished letters of G. B. Gelli on the Comedy of Dante], Florence, 1887 ; *Lezioni di B. Varchi sul Dante*, ecc. [Readings of B. Varchi on Dante, etc.], Florence, 1841.

[4] In an appendix to the above-cited book of Barbi.

[5] *Sposizione di Lodovico Castelvetro a XXIX canti dell' Inferno* [Exposition of Lodovico Castelvetro to XXIX Cantos of the Inferno], Modena, 1886.

that century we have, besides the *Indici* [Indices] of Volpi,[1] the commentaries of Pompeo Venturi and of Francesco Baldassarre Lombardi; the first[2] aims to explain merely the literal sense, and is very concise (and not seldom, truly lean); the second, which has served as foundation to very many subsequent interpreters,[3] while it does not lack erroneous explanations, gives new light on many passages, and properly holds in equal balance the letter and the allegory.

Among the many, even too many, commentaries of the nineteenth century, let us recall the most worthy, assigning the first place to that of Tommaso Casini,[4] eclectic but carried out with rare prudence (especially in the historical part), and to another, by G. A. Scartazzini, likewise eclectic, far more extended, but not so well proportioned in its various parts nor as judicious and coherent in its accepted or proposed explanations. The latter work gradually expanded in the author's hands, so that the third

---

[1] *Indici ricchissimi che spiegano tutte le cose difficili e tutte le erudizioni del poema e tengono la vece d' un intero comento* [Very Full Indices which explain All the Difficult and Erudite Things in the Poem and take the Place of a Full Commentary], Padua, 1727 (in the third volume of the Comino edition of the *Commedia*).

[2] *La Div. Comm. con una breve e sufficiente dichiarazione del senso letterale, diversa in più luoghi da quella degli antichi comentatori (del P. Pompeo Venturi)* [The Divine Comedy with a Short and Adequate Explanation of the Literal Sense (by P. Pompeo Venturi)], Verona, 1749 (this is the first complete edition of this commentary).

[3] *La Div. Comm. novamente corretta, spiegata e difesa da F. B. L. M. C.* [The Divine Comedy newly corrected, explained, and defended by F. B. L. M. C.], Rome, 1791. Two others follow the footsteps of this commentator in the beginning of the next century: Lugi Portirelli (Milan, 1804–1805) and Gaetano Poggiali (Leghorn, 1807–1813). Giosafatte Biagioli, too, in his *Commento alla Div. Comm.* [Commentary to the Divine Comedy], which he published at Paris in 1818–1819, availed himself of it not infrequently, although he often censured it.

[4] Fifth edition, enlarged and corrected, Florence, 1903.

volume is twice the size of the first.[1] Scartazzini has also given us a " smaller edition " of his Commentary, much improved by G. Vandelli in the fifth reprint.[2] In addition we may profitably use even now the commentaries of Paolo Costa,[3] of Brunone Bianchi,[4] of Pietro Fraticelli,[5] of Raffaele Andreoli,[6] of Eugenio Camerini,[7] all of a volume and character befitting students of and beginners in these studies. The comments on the *Commedia* by Niccolò Tommaseo (full of discernment and useful as well for the knowledge of the philosophic thought of Alighieri) have especial importance for æsthetic considerations ; [8] for the theological doctrines, those of the Fathers Gio. Maria Cornoldi,[9] Gioachino Berthier,[10] Domenico Palmieri,[11] and of Mons. Giacomo Poletto.[12] Antonio Lubin[13] paraphrased the *Commedia* in prose, prefacing it with ample " preparatory explanatory studies " and accompanying it with a commentary ; Giuseppi Campi[14] added " notes published and unpublished, ancient and modern " to a text of the poem based (but with insufficient critical acumen) on some sixty codices and old printed editions.

[1] Leipzig, 1874–1882. The first volume was afterwards reprinted by the author with considerable additions and a *Concordanza della Div. Comm.* [Concordance of the Divine Comedy], which is also found separately (Leipzig, 1900).

[2] Milan, 1907 (with corrected dictionary of rimes by L. Polacco).

[3] Naples, 1830 (reprinted several times).

[4] Florence, 1854 (reprinted several times). It is the *Dante* of the Le Monnier collection.   [5] Florence, 1852 (reprinted several times).

[6] Naples, 1856 (reprinted several times).

[7] Milan, 1868–1869 (with illustrations by Doré). Cheap edition, Milan, 1873 (reprinted several times).

[8] Venice, 1837 (reprinted several times). P. Antonio Cesari made the gems of language with which the poem sparkles, shine before our eyes (*Bellezze della Comm. di D. A.*, Verona, 1824–1826).   [9] Rome, 1887.

[10] Fribourg (Switzerland), 1892–1897 (commentary to the *Inferno* alone).   [11] Prato, 1898–1899.

[12] Rome-Tournay, 1894.   [13] Padua, 1881.   [14] Turin, 1888–1891.

4. Fame and imitations of the poem from the fourteenth to the sixteenth century. The high and universal admiration which, from the fourteenth century to our days, was aroused in Italy by the Dantesque masterpiece, together with the expository literature, is testified to by the praise bestowed upon it and the imitations of it which were made. All these latter were more or less disastrous! Dante, I say with Giosue Carducci, "descended from Paradise bringing with him the keys of the otherworld, and threw them into the abyss of the past. No one has ever found them again." It will be well to call these imitations to mind, however, by telling briefly the story of the fortune of our poem in Italy.

Dante's fame, already diffused when he died, spread rapidly. In the third decennial of the fourteenth century there appeared the first commentaries on the poem. In 1373 Boccaccio was named as its public expounder ; the *Commedia* was explained in the churches ; Dante chairs were founded in the various cities of Italy.[1] And soon Alighieri's masterpiece began to be imitated, as well. These imitations, however, are in nowise worthy of the greatest of our writers. The *Dottrinale* [Doctrinal] of his son Jacopo is a very poor affair ! Fazio degli Uberti, great-grandson of Farinata, under the title of *Dittamondo*, gathers all that was told of the world (*dicta mundi*), pretending to journey through it guided by the old geographer Solinus, in a poem in *terza rima* full of Dantesque reminiscences,

---

[1] Adverse criticism was not lacking. Francesco Stabili, better known under the name of Cecco d'Ascoli (d. 1327), cast blame upon Alighieri with dogmatic superciliousness, and accused him of heresy in an uncouth and dry poem, couched in turbid language, named the *Acerba* (as if to denote a *bitter* thing, that is, "difficult to understand"). The stanzas of this poem, of six lines, are a transformation of Dante's *terzine*.

in which he merely enumerates places and historical facts, when he is not engaged in putting Solinian treatises into verse. In the *Quadriregio* Federico Frezzi of Foligno, at the end of the fourteenth century, has given us (always in *terzine*, and taking from Dante imagery, images, and lines) a vast aggregation of allegories and symbolic personifications, confused and abstruse, in the form of a journey through the four kingdoms of Love, Satana, the Vices, and the Virtues. In which poem he, a Dominican theologue and bishop of his city from 1403, has sacrificed poetry to the philosophic and doctrinal content. This happens, also, in two other poems in imitation of Dante, written about the same time : the *Fimerodia* of Jacopo del Pecora of Montepulciano (who composed it in glorification of virtuous love, between 1390 and 1397) and the *Pietosa fonte* [Pitiful Spring] of Zenone of Pistoia (an apotheosis of Petrarch, who was personally known by the author). And not much better, although indeed less vapid as concerns its art, is the *Amorosa visione* [Amorous Vision] (1342) of Boccaccio : fifty cantos in *terzine*, in which the *Commedia* is freely imitated, and in which we see female loveliness represented (just as in Dante) as an instrument of the soul's regeneration.[1] Not much better, if we leave out of consideration the very beautiful description of Laura's death, are the *Trionfi* [Triumphs], in which Petrarch, during the last years of his life (from 1357 on), wished to glorify his beloved lady, imitating the great

[1] The *Amorosa visione* [Amorous Vision] is, like the *Commedia*, allegoric. And a moral allegory (the perfecting of man by means of the cardinal and theological virtues personified in seven nymphs) is found also in the *Ameto* of the same Boccaccio (1341 or 1342), in which short cantos in *terza rima*, not without frequent reminiscences of Dante, are inserted in the prose story of the loves of Ameto and Lia.

work of Alighieri in exaltation of Beatrice, in the same meter and with an analogous visionary and symbolic content.
The moral precepts and the enumerations of historic personages with which it overflows are more appropriate to a
treatise or a chronicle than to a poem.

In the fifteenth century the study of Dante declined.
We have, indeed, other poems of the type of the *Commedia:* the anonymous *Leandreide*, written between 1420 and
1429, the *Città di vita* [City of Life] by Matteo Palmieri,
and the *Giardino* [Garden] by Marino Jonata of Agnone
(both composed between 1455 and 1465), the *Visione*
[Vision] by Gambino d' Arezzo (1475 *ca.*) ; and there
are not lacking hardy spirits devoted to the great Tuscan
triumvirate of the fourteenth century, like that Giovanni
Gherardi of Prato (the author of the *Paradiso degli Alberti*
[Paradise of the Alberti]), who was a public expounder
of Dante and imitated the latter in a certain poem of
his. But the fanaticism for classic antiquity caused the
maternal tongue and its glories to be neglected by many.

The restoration of the *Commedia* to honor was the
greatest title to glory for Italian criticism at the end of
the fifteenth century [1] and the first half of the sixteenth.
At least fifteen editions of the *Commedia* appeared in
the last twenty-eight years of the fifteenth century alone,
and forty in the sixteenth, thirty-four of which have been
verified. Eminent scholars set to work to purge the principal work of Alighieri from the damage wrought upon it
by ignorant scribes, or to explain its manifold doctrine
and its subtle concepts. Poets such as Ariosto and Tasso,

---

[1] Of this period (1493 and later) there is also a noteworthy poem
in imitation of the *Commedia*, — the *Anima peregrina* [Pilgrim Soul]
of Tommaso de' Sardi.

artists like Michael Angelo, literary men of true worth like Varchi, Gelli, Tríssino, Speroni, warmly admired the *Commedia*, which, in the edition of 1555, printed by Gabriel Giolito and brothers, first bore on its title-page that title of *divine*, which it has always retained. In the Florentine Academy, where it was the custom to expound Dante, and where Varchi, when he was consul of it in 1545, gave thirteen readings on the first two cantos of the *Paradiso*, Giambattista Gelli, appointed in 1553 by the duke Cosimo to expound publicly the *Commedia*, whenever he came across passages censured by Dante's adversaries, consistently repelled the accusations. Furthermore Alighieri's part was taken by many others, among them that clear-sighted and clear-headed philologue, Vincenzio Borghini, and Jacopo Mazzoni of Cesena, who, in 1587, published in an emended form a detailed *Difesa della Commedia* [Defense of the *Commedia*].

If to the writings on the divine poem in a critical and polemical vein we add the attempts to amend its text which were made by many, especially at Florence (the studies of Giambullari, Vellutello, and others concerning the site, the form, and the measurements of the Dantesque hell; the lectures on the *Commedia* which were given at Florence, Verona, Genoa, Milan, Venice, Padua; partial or complete commentaries of the poem; and, finally, the important annotations of Borghini scattered through note-books, as yet in manuscript only, and in his copy of the *Commedia*), we must conclude with Cesare Balbo that the sixteenth century " was for Dante a century of increasing and extending glory." Nor shall we be astonished at the imitations of the poem which were made at this period by Carlo de' Ludovici in his *Trionfi di Carlo* [Triumphs of

Charles], by Machiavelli in his *Asino d'oro* [Golden Ass], by Giovanni Filoteo Achillini in his *Fedele* [Faithful One], by Zanobi Ceffini in his *Peregrinazione* [Pilgrimage], by an anonymous writer in the poem *Della diffusione del sommo bene* [On the Diffusion of the Supreme Good], and by Francesco Porta in his *Visione*[1] [Vision], just as we shall not be astonished at the power which the Dantesque poetry exercised over the art of Buonarroti and other noted painters and sculptors of that age.

5. Fame of the poem in the seventeenth and eighteenth centuries. In the next century, the seventeenth, the corruption of taste and the weakening of thought hindered most people from enjoying Dante's masterpiece. And the strictures upon the latter grew harsher and received a greater circulation, especially after the publication, in 1608, of the *Discorso nel quale si mostra l' imperfezione della Commedia* [Discourse in which the Imperfection of the *Commedia* is Shown Forth] (a widely circulated manuscript of about 1571), which is shown to be the handiwork of Leonardo Salviati. Grammarians and rhetoricians are now scandalized at this or that word used by Alighieri ; now they compare one of his lines or passages with a like one of Vergil or Homer, trying to show his inferiority ; now they accuse him " of having offended this or that standard of the Stagyrite, consecrated by the Latin and Greek epics."

As is natural, there were not lacking men who ridiculed such callow censures. Boccalini, in his *Ragguagli di Parnaso* [Notices of Parnassus], tells of an onset made upon

[1] In the volume *Dai tempi antichi ai tempi moderni*, ecc. [From Ancient to Modern Times, etc.] (published in honor of the Scherillo-Negri marriage), Milan, 1904, pp. 407–416, I showed that Porta gave out, without the least scruple, as his own that which he took wholesale from the *Commedia*.

Dante by three men in disguise, to make him declare
whether his poem is a comedy, a tragi-comedy, or an epic.
But the strong, the untrammeled minds inclined before
that great one, even in the seventeenth century. Thus
Galileo, his admirer, in two lectures explained and commented upon the opinions of Antonio Manetti and Alessandro Vellutello on the shape and site of the Inferno.
Magalotti, who visited with devotion and emotion the
poet's tomb at Ravenna, judiciously elucidated the first
five cantos of the first cantica. Redi in his writings shows
a great veneration for that " most grand mind (these are his
words) which knew everything, and knew how to write of
everything so marvelously." Praises of Dante are not lacking, moreover, in lyrics and poems of that age. An ecclesi-
astic of the Veneto, Toldo Costantini, exalted it to heaven
in a long sacred poem in *ottava rima*, *Del giudicio estremo*
[Of the Last Judgment], which he declares in the title itself
to be "composed in imitation of Dante." But these are oa-
ses in the desert ! The fact remains that from 1596 to 1702
we have only three editions of the *Commedia*, and no commentary ; that the seventeenth century has given us nothing on the life and works of Alighieri except "many trifles
of grammarians or little more " ; that a bookish friar, who
reflects very faithfully in his writings the tendencies of his
century, dared to exclaim, enraged by the praises bestowed
upon the sacred poem: "Body of Dante ! It 's a great joke
that he, with his worn-out hood, should have unhooded so
many, while he makes many slips in comparison with the
numerous writers who wrote more divinely than he." [1]

[1] [The point of this passage lies in the use of the word *scappucciare*,
which means both to take off one's hood and to make slips.]

Fr. Fulvio Frugoni, *Ritratti critici* [Critical Portraits], Venice, 1669,
iii, 369-373. And the good man continues: "As for me (fortunate

Better fortune smiled on the Dante cult in the eighteenth century. Alighieri had in this century most fervid admirers, especially in Verona, where Giovanni Jacopo Dionisi published on Dante a *Serie di aneddoti* [Series of Anecdotes] (1785–1794 and 1806), making of himself "the instigator of a new criticism" on the poet's works. The editions of the *Commedia* multiply; "eulogies of Dante" and verses in his praise are composed (especially noteworthy is the sonnet of Vittorio Alfieri before the poet's tomb); with a few exceptions, our most noteworthy writers of this age "looked — to say it with Crescimbeni — towards the *Commedia*, as towards the principal foundation of the Tuscan language, no less than of poetry." [1]

There were not lacking, however, even in this period of literary revival, censors of Dante intent upon inflicting on him the usual reproach of being obscure or harsh. And, with more authority than any others, the Mantuan Jesuit, Saverio Bettinelli, in his *Lettere dieci di Virgilio agli Arcadi* [Ten Letters of Vergil to the Arcadians] (edited, together with the famous *Versi sciolti di tre eccellenti autori* [Blank Verse of Three Excellent Authors], in 1757), reviled Alighieri and his admirers and imitators, pretending that Vergil, from the Elysian Fields where the ancient poets are gathered together, refers their discussions to the Academy of Arcadia. These *Lettere virgiliane* [Vergilian Letters] made a stir; and as, then and afterwards, there were those who applauded the rebellion of Bettinelli against a decree sanctioned by general consent (in France,

fellow!), I esteem more highly, and I am sure of not being mistaken, a verse of the odes of Vidali, of Saltinelli, of Ciampoli, of Testi, of Balducci, of Stampa, of Dottori, and of other great lyric poets of our time, than all the *Commedia*."

[1] Cf. what Vico, Alfieri, Muratori, Zeno, Gravina, Maffei, efc. thought of it.

Voltaire ; with us, among others, Cesarotti),[1] just so there promptly arose to repel these accusations that sagacious and witty writer, Gaspare Gozzi. He, in the so-called *Difesa di Dante* [Defense of Dante], that is, in the *Giudizio degli antichi poeti sopra la moderna censura di Dante attribuita ingiustamente a Virgilio* [Judgment of the Ancient Poets upon the Modern Censure of Dante attributed unjustly to Vergil], which he printed in 1758, confutes with method, with exactness of logic, with happy arguments, the affirmations of Bettinelli and of all those who denied " good taste " to Alighieri, and yet conceded him what, according to the fashion of the times, was called " genius."

If to this we add the other protests or refutations to which these notorious letters gave occasion, if we add the replies which the unjust and violent strictures of Voltaire received, even on the part of those who, like Baretti, were not most favorably disposed to Dante, we must conclude that the eighteenth century was, taken all in all, an age of auspicious fortune for Alighieri and his great work.

6. The cult of Dante and the state of the studies on the *Commedia* in our times. But the true "age of Dante," as regards the heartfelt cult accorded to the poet, was that just elapsed.

Already in the second half of the eighteenth century the exterior forms of the *Commedia* had been imitated by Alfonso Varano in the *Visioni* [Visions] and by Vincenzo Monti in the *Bassvilliana* [Poem of Bassville].

---

[1] The latter, writing to Bettinelli after having read his *Dissertazione accademica sopra Dante* [Academic Dissertation on Dante], which appeared just at the close of the century, defined the poem as a "grotesque hodgepodge, which can be truly called a non-divine Comedy."

In the nineteenth century Luigi Grisostomo Ferrucci composed the *Scala di vita* [Ladder of Life] in imitation of Dante's poem ; Monti himself stimulated, by his precepts as well as by his very authoritative example, the study of the masterpiece ; Ugo Foscolo wrote an extended discourse, *Sul testo della Divina Commedia* [On the Text of the Divine Comedy], which is among the best of his critical writings. And almost all the most distinguished writers of the time were students of the poem : notably Manzoni, Tommaseo, Giusti, Niccolini, Leopardi. The latter, in his ode on the monument to Dante to be erected in Florence, exclaimed, turning towards the poet :

> [if e'er thou didst,
> if ever thou shalt fall from out our mind,
> may our ill greater grow, an can it grow ;
> obscure to all mankind
> may thy stock weep, in everlasting woe.]

There wrote on the *Commedia* (besides the above-mentioned commentators) Perticari, Balbo, Gioberti, Rossetti, Borghi, Centofanti, etc., and, in the second half of that century and the first years of the present one, Fr. Perez, De Sanctis, Carducci, D'Ancona, Del Lungo, Graf, D'Ovidio, Tocco, Chiappelli, Pascoli, and many other writers of worth. As in 1865 the centennial of Dante's birth, so in 1900 the centennial of his visionary journey gave occasion for the most varied publications. G. B. Giuliani, the well-known advocate of the method of "explaining Dante by Dante," held a chair of Dante at Florence. At the present time Alessandro D'Ancona expounds Dante at the University of Pisa, as does Giacomo Poletto in the papal "Istituto Leoniano d'alta letteratura." And even outside of Italy the *Commedia* has had, and has, most

zealous students ; as in Germany, King John of Saxony
(Philalethes), Witte, Blanc, Ruth, Hettinger, Kraus, Bassermann ; in England, Plumptre, W. Warren Vernon,
Moore, Toynbee, Wicksteed, Gardner; in France, Ozanam
and Fauriel ; in Switzerland, Scartazzini. I merely mention the Dante societies founded on both sides of the
ocean,[1] the astounding Dante library got together by
Willard Fiske, an American, and presented by him to
Cornell University, the translations of the *Commedia* that
exist in almost every language and that are multiplying
rapidly in the principal tongues of Europe. Suffice it to
observe that America has, in the Dante cult, associated herself with Germany and England, as the remarkable translations of Longfellow and Norton testify ; that in Italy the
Commedia is to-day publicly expounded in all the large
cities, read in all cultivated families, regarded by all as
the national book, pride of the Latin race.

And the seriousness with which we have now begun to
study it is attested especially by the pains taken critically
to reconstruct the original text.

As every one knows, the autograph of the poem has not
come down to us ; indeed, we do not possess even a single
word written in his own hand by Alighieri. Therefore
scientific criticism, wishing to establish a text of the *Commedia* as near as possible to that which was penned by
the author, must work over the manuscripts, in which it
has been preserved to us in such a profuse variety of

[1] [The Dante Society of America has published two invaluable con-
cordances, of the Inferno by Fay and of the minor Italian works by
Sheldon and White. It issues an annual report (the last is the twenty-
sixth) in which [articles of interest are to be found, aids the Dante
Collection in the Library of Harvard University, and offers an annual
prize for the best essay on Dantesque subjects. It will soon publish a
concordance to the Latin works, by Rand and White.]

readings. These manuscripts are very numerous; from the fourth decade of the fourteenth century to the end of the fifteenth we can count more than five hundred.[1] Hence the necessity of proceeding according to the most scientific standards of philological principles.

Such a study began to be followed seriously in the nineteenth century. In 1862 a meritorious German student of Dante, Carl Witte, gave out the text of the poem revised upon the codices, giving an account of his work in the learned and judicious " prolegomeni." [2] In 1889 Edward Moore, an English student of Dante still living, published a complete collation of the whole of the *Inferno* based on eighteen manuscripts, and a collation of one hundred and fifty chosen passages made from a larger number of codices, discussing the various readings, determining the causes of alterations in the written texts, pointing out the difficulties met with in the interpretation of manuscripts and the aid which may be obtained for the critical study of the text from the classical reminiscences which occur in Dante.[3] The question of the proper method to be followed in the difficult undertaking was raised by

[1] We should recall, among the earliest and most celebrated, the codex of S. Croce (also called the codex Villani), the "Gaddiano," and the two "Tempiani," (formerly belonging to the Marquis Tempi), all of these in the Royal Medicean-Laurentian Library of Florence; the codex "Poggiali," in the Royal National Central Library of the same city; the so-called codex of Petrarch, in the Apostolic Vatican Library of Rome (No. 3199); the codex "Landiano," in the Passerini-Landi Library of Piacenza; the Este codex, in the Royal Este Library of Modena; the " Trivulziano," in the Library of Prince Trivulzio of Milan (No. 2); the "Bartoliniano," in the Bartolinian Library of Udine, etc.

[2] *La Divina Commedia di Dante Alighieri ricorretta sopra quattro dei più autorevoli testi a penna* [The Divine Comedy of Dante Alighieri corrected on Four of the Most Authoritative Codices], Berlin, 1862.

[3] *Contributions to the textual criticism of the Divina Commedia,* Cambridge, 1889.

many, with a variety of ideas and propositions; attempts were made, not without some fruit, albeit premature; in their study of the subject some arrived at conclusions which may not be neglected. But though the possibility of forming a true and legitimate genealogical tree for the codices which have come down to us has been excluded, it has been shown to be feasible to separate them into families, in order to determine the relations between the various " manuscript traditions." To such an end it should be recognized as necessary to compare the different codices as a whole, and not as regards a chosen number of places, so as not to neglect, to the detriment of the final result, any of those elements upon which the solution of the problem must necessarily be founded.[1]

The direction of the work by which we may hope that Italy shall one day possess a truly national edition of its poem is, by the judicious opinion of the Società Dantesca Italiana [Italian Dante Society], in the hands of Pio Rajna. And one of his students has recently published a text of the *Commedia* based on " a series of old codices judged to be of particular importance, and all submitted to minute and accurate recensions," [2] which may be considered as of the highest promise of what students confidently await from him and from his distinguished master.

Moreover, the Società Dantesca, founded at Florence in 1888, has not only given its attention to this work, but has

[1] Cf. Barbi, *Per il testo della Divina Commedia* [As to the Text of the Divine Comedy], Rome, 1891 (extract from the *Rivista critica della letteratura italiana* [Critical Review of Italian Literature], years vi and vii).

[2] *La Divina Commedia di Dante Alighieri novamente illustrata da artisti italiani* [The Divine Comedy of Dante Alighieri newly illustrated by Italian Artists], Florence, Fratelli Alinari, 1902 et seq. The editor is Professor G. Vandelli, who exposes in his preface the standards followed in the reconstitution of the text.

instituted in the same city a public interpretation of the poem in the hall of Or San Michele ; besides correlating the studies of Italian and foreign scholars on Dante, reducing to order the exegetic work on the *Commedia* and the Opere Minori (in which, to a too great degree, even the unprepared and presumptuous take part in great numbers), combating the revival of opinions already shown to be erroneous, and defending, by restraining the arbitrary minds, the surely acquired patrimony of knowledge. Its *Bullettino*, intelligently conducted, formerly by M. Barbi and now by E. G. Parodi, looks to all this. And all those who study seriously the poem that all the world admires, seem convinced of one thing, and that is, that it is not possible to come to the end of anything, either as regards the æsthetic analysis or in reference to the understanding of the fundamental thought of a work as complex as the *Commedia*, if we do not follow that scientific method which criticism has, for our good fortune, long since established in Italy.

APPENDIX

AIDS TO THE STUDY OF DANTE'S *COMMEDIA*

I

BIBLIOGRAPHIES

C. DE BATINES, *Bibliografia dantesca, ossia Catalogo delle edizioni, traduzioni, codici e commenti della Divina Commedia e delle opere minori di Dante*, etc., Prato, 1845–1848, 3 vols. (see also the *Giunte e correzioni ined.* to this Bibliography, Florence, 1888, and the *Indice generale* to it, Bologna, 1883).

J. FERRAZZI, *Manuale dantesco*, Bassano, 1871–1877, 5 vols.

G. PETZHOLDT, *Bibliographia Dantea*, Dresden, 1876–1880.

W. C. LANE, The Dante. Collections in the Harvard College and Boston Public Libraries, Cambridge, Mass., 1890.

G. A. SCARTAZZINI, *Dante in Germania*, Milan, 1881–1883, 2 vols. (a catalogue of German publications on Dante). A *Supplemento* (1883–1893) in the *Giornale dantesco*, I, 174–187.

TH. W. KOCH, Catalogue of the Dante Collection presented by Willard Fiske, Ithaca, New York, 1898–1900, 2 vols. (a work of fundamental importance).

G. L. PASSERINI and C. MAZZI, *Un decennio di bibliografia dantesca (1891–1900)*, Milan, 1905.

II

DICTIONARIES, CONCORDANCES, ENCYCLOPEDIAS

L. G. BLANC, *Vocabolario dantesco*, etc., Florence, 1859 (translated from the French, Leipzig, 1852).

E. A. FAY, Concordance of the *Divina Commedia*, Cambridge, Mass., 1888.

E. S. Sheldon and A. C. White, *Concordanza delle opere italiane in prosa e del canzoniere di Dante Alighieri*, Oxford, 1905.

G. Poletto, *Dizionario dantesco di quanto si contiene nelle opere di D. A., con richiami alla Somma teologica di S. Tommaso d'Aquino, coll'illustrazione dei nomi proprî mitologici, storici, geografici, e delle questioni piú controverse*, Siena, 1885–1892, 7 vols. and an Appendix.

G. A. Scartazzini, *Enciclopedia dantesca: Dizionario critico e ragionato di quanto concerne la vita e le opere di D. A.*, Milan, 1896–1899, Vols. I and II.

A. Fiammazzo, *Enciclopedia dantesca di G. A. Scartazzini continuata*, Vol. III: *Vocabolario-Concordanza delle opere latine e italiane di D. A.*, ibid. 1905.

P. Toynbee, A Dictionary of Proper Names and Notable Matters in the Works of Dante, Oxford, 1898 (a very important work).[1]

III

PERIODICALS

L'Alighieri, edited by F. Pasqualigo, Verona, 1889–1892, 4 vols.

Giornale dantesco, edited by G. L. Passerini, Venice and later Florence, 1893–1910, 18 vols.

Bullettino della Società dantesca italiana, edited by M. Barbi and later by E. G. Parodi, Florence, 1890–1910, Series I (bibliography of works on Dante) and Series II (critical survey of studies on Dante. It contains also the proceedings of the society).

Bibliografia dantesca: Rassegna bibliografica degli studî intorno a Dante, al Trecento e a cose francescane, edited by L. Suttina, 1902–1905, 2 vols.

Lectura Dantis, Florence, 1900–1910 (cantos of the *Divina Commedia* read and explained by various scholars in Or San Michele).[2]

---

[1] For a *Concordanza della D. C.* compiled by Scartazzini, see supra, p. 121, note 1.

[2] Thus, since the Dante lectures in Or San Michele are continued, in time we shall have a complete commentary on the poem by Dantologists from every part of Italy. The first twenty-three cantos, commented on in public in Genoa by various scholars, are printed under the title "*Lectura Dantis*" *genovese*, Florence, 1904, 1906.

Collezione di opuscoli danteschi inediti o rari, edited by G. L. Passerini, Città di Castello, 1893–1910.

Biblioteca storico-critica della letteratura dantesca, founded by G. L. Passerini and P. Papa, now edited by P. Papa, Bologna, 1899–1905.

IV

BOOKS OF PRIME IMPORTANCE ON THE *COMMEDIA*

G. B. GIULIANI, *Metodo di commentare la Commedia di D. A.*, Florence, 1861.

E. RUTH, *Studî sopra D. A. per servire all'intelligenza della D. C.*, Venice and Turin, 1865, 2 vols. (translated from the German).

G. TODESCHINI, *Scritti su Dante*, Vicenza, 1872, 2 vols. (the first is completely dedicated to the poem).

A. BARTOLI, *La Divina Commedia*, Vol. VI (in two parts) in the *Storia della letteratura italiana*, Florence, 1887–1889.

I. DEL LUNGO, *Dante ne' tempi di Dante*, Bologna, 1888, and *Dal secolo e dal poema di D.*, ibid. 1898.

L. LEYNARDI, *La psicologia dell'arte nella D. C.*, Turin, 1894.

E. MOORE, Studies on Dante, First Series, Oxford, 1896; Second Series, ibid. 1899; Third Series, ibid. 1903.

F. D'OVIDIO, *Studî sulla D. C.*, Milan-Palermo, 1901.

F. D'OVIDIO, *Nuovi studî danteschi*, Milan, 1907.[1]

P. TOYNBEE, Dante Studies and Researches, London, 1902.

A. BASSERMANN, *Orme di Dante in Italia*, Bologna, 1902 (translated from the German).[2]

[1] Noteworthy collections of articles or studies on Dante are also those of V. Capetti (Leghorn, 1907), G. Federzoni (Bologna), N. Scarano (Leghorn, 1905), A. Chiappelli (Florence, 1905), etc.

[2] We may further profitably consult the *Dante* of F. S. Kraus, Berlin, 1897, especially that part treating of the *Commedia*, and the work of N. Zingarelli, Milan, 1903. Many notes may be found, as well, in the recent work of F. Torraca, Rome-Milan, 1905 et seq. A general study on the philosophic genesis of the poem is the very recent work of K. Vossler, *Die gottliche Komödie*, Heidelberg, 1907 et seq.

V

BOOKS DESCRIBING THE THREE DANTESQUE KINGDOMS

MICHELANGELO CAETANI, *La materia della D. C. dichiarata in VI tavole*, Rome, 1855; ibid. 1872 (splendid edition); Florence, 1886 (cheap edition).

G. AGNELLI, *Topocronografia del viaggio dantesco*, Milan, 1891.

M. PORENA, *Commento grafico alla D. C.*, Milan-Palermo-Naples, 1902.

E. MOORE, *Gli accenni al tempo nella D. C.*, etc., Florence, 1900 (translated from the English). It is No. 32 in the *Biblioteca critica della letteratura italiana*, published by Sansoni.

F. D'OVIDIO, *Nuovi studî danteschi: il Purgatorio e il suo preludio*, Milan, 1906.

P. PEREZ, *I sette cerchi del Purgatorio di D.*, Verona, 1867.

E. COLI, *Il Paradiso terrestre dantesco*, Florence, 1897.

T. BOTTAGISIO, *Il Limbo dantesco*, Padua, 1898.

G. PASCOLI, *Minerva oscura*, Leghorn, 1898 (on the moral classification of the *Inferno* and the *Purgatorio*).[1]

G. BUSNELLI, *L'Etica Nicomachea — la Divina Commedia*, Bologna, 1906, in the *Biblioteca della letteratura dantesca*, edited by P. Papa.

G. BUSNELLI, *La concezione del Purgatorio dantesco*, Rome, 1906.

VI

THE BEST KNOWN EDITIONS OF THE POEM

There are about 425 editions of the *Commedia* from 1472 to 1900. Of these, 15 date from before the sixteenth century, 34 are of that century, 3 are of the seventeenth, 31 of the eighteenth, and 342 of the nineteenth century.

We may mention as the most noteworthy the four earliest (reprinted at the expense of G. G. Warren Vernon at London, 1858): Foligno, 1472, Mantua, 1472, Jesi, 1472, Naples, 1474; the Vindelinani

---

[1] Pascoli is about to publish his general exposition of the poem, of which he has printed two volumes (*Sotto il velame*, Messina, 1900, and *La mirabile visione*, ibid. 1902).

(Venice, Vendelin da Spira, 1477); the Nidobeatine (Milan, M. P. Nidobeato, 1477–1478); the first Florentine edition (Niccolò della Magna, 1481); the two Aldine (1502 and 1515), and the Giuntine of 1506; the Venetian edition, Giolíto, 1555, edited by Lodovico Dolce; that of the della Crusca (Florence, 1595), edited by Bastiano de'Rossi, secretary of this Academy, and some of his colleagues; the Cominian, edited and furnished with indexes by Gio. Ant. Volpi (Padua, 1726–1727); that of the Zatta (Venice, 1757–1758) with "copious engravings," dedicated to the "Empress of all the Russias";[1] the magnificent Bodinian (Parma, 1795); the Pisan of 1804–1809, edited by Rosini, and the Livornese of 1807–1813, edited by Poggiali; that of Milan, 1809, in large format, and that other, splendidly printed and with copperplates, which appeared in Florence, at the Sign of the Anchor, from 1817 to 1819; the edition of Minerva (Padua, 1822), very correct and praiseworthy, reprinted several times; that of Udine (1823–1828), based on the Bartolinian codex; the Le Monnier edition (Florence, 1837), supervised by Niccolini, Capponi, Borghi, and Fruttuoso Becchi, and the other, with notes by Ugo Foscolo, which appeared at London in 1842–1843; that edited by Karl Witte (Berlin, 1862) with careful attention to a critical text; the Milanese microscopic edition of 1878 (the so-called "Dantino"), printed at Padua by Salmin.[2]

To the last ten years of the last century belong the *Divina Commedia ridotta a miglior lezione*, etc., by G. Campi, Turin, 1888–1891, the *Divina Commedia illustrata nei luoghi e nelle persone* by C. Ricci, Milan, 1896–1897 (with 430 illustrations), and the *Divina Commedia nuovamente riveduta nel testo* by E. Moore, Oxford, 1900 (with an index of proper names compiled by Toynbee); all three editions important in various ways. From 1902 to 1904 V. Alinari published in Florence the *Divina Commedia novamente illustrata da artisti italiani*, with critical text by G. Vandelli.

---

[1] This is the first fully illustrated edition. For later illustrated editions, see L. Volkmann, *Iconografia dantesca*, Florence, 1898 (translated from the German).

[2] The Dantino of Barbèra of Florence (1898) is very small, but not microscopic and hence more practical. Judiciously annotated pocket editions are those of G. L. Passerini, Florence, 1897–1901, and of R. Fornaciari, Milan, 1904.

VII

TRANSLATIONS

Neglecting the partial translations, which are very numerous, let us note here the principal ones of the whole poem.

In Bohemian the *Commedia* was translated by J. VRCHLICKÝ (Prague, 1879–1882);

In Catalan by A. FEBRER (fifteenth century; printed in Barcelona, 1878);

In Danish by C. MOLBECH (Copenhagen, 1851–1862);

In Dutch by A. S. KOK (Haarlem, 1863–1864), by J. C. HACKE VAN MIJNDEN (ibid. 1867–1873), by U. W. THODEN VAN VELZEN (Leeuwarden, 1874–1875), by J. BOHL (Haarlem, 1876–1885);

In English by E. BOYD (London, 1802), by H. F. CARY (ibid. 1814; very often reprinted, the last time, ibid. 1900–1902), by J. C. WRIGHT (London, 1833–1840), by H. W. LONGFELLOW (Boston, 1867; very often reprinted, for example at London in 1893), by E. H. PLUMPTRE (ibid. 1886–1887), by A. J. BUTLER (ibid. 1880–1892), by C. E. NORTON (Boston, 1891–1892), by T. W. PARSONS (ibid. 1893), by F. K. H. HASELFOOT (London, 1887); by W. WARREN VERNON (London, 1894–1897);[1]

In French by B. GRANGIER (Paris, 1596), by COLBERT D'ES-TOUTEVILLE (ibid. 1796), by A. F. ARTAUD (ibid. 1811–1813), by P. A. FIORENTINO (ibid. 1841),[2] by A. BRIZEUX (ibid. 1842), by P. AROUX (ibid. 1842), by S. G. DE CESENA (ibid. 1843–1846), by F. DE LAMENNAIS (ibid. 1855), by L. RATISBONNE (ibid. 1856 et seq.), by J. A. MONGIS (Dijon, 1857), by J. A. MESNARD (Paris,

---

[1] The translation of Vernon is in his important work, Readings on the *Inferno*, *Purgatorio*, and *Paradiso* (in 6 vols.). Koch notes nine other complete English translations, but of less value, in his Catalogue of the Collection of W. Fiske, I, 42–49. To these we should add that in prose by H. F. Tozer (Oxford, 1904); see the *Bullettino della Società dantesca italiana*, N. S., XII, 231–233, and cf. Toynbee, A Chronological List of English Translations of Dante, in the Twenty-fourth Annual Report of the Dante Society of America (Cambridge, Mass., 1905).

[2] This translation was reprinted in an *édition de luxe* with Doré's illustrations (Paris, 1861–1868).

1854–1857), by M. Durand Fardel (ibid. 1895; free translation), by A. de Margérie (Paris, 1900);[1]

In German by L. Bachenschwanz (Hamburg and Leipzig, 1767–1769), by C. L. Kannegiesser (Leipzig, 1814–1821; often reprinted), by C. Streckfuss (Halle, 1824–1826; often reprinted), by King John of Saxony, under the name of Phillaethes (Dresden and Leipzig, 1840 et seq.; often reprinted), by A. Kopisch (Berlin, 1837–1842), by L. G. Blanc (Halle, 1864), by C. Witte (Berlin, 1865), by C. Bartsch (Leipzig, 1877), by G. Francke (Leipzig, 1883–1885), by O. Gildemeister (Berlin, 1888), by C. Bertrand (Heidelberg, 1887–1894), by P. Pochhammer (Leipzig, 1901; free translation), etc.;[2]

In Greek (modern) by G. E. Antoniades (Athens, 1881), and by C. Musurus Pasha (London, 1882–1885);

In Hungarian by C. Szász (Budapest, 1885–1891);[3]

In Latin by the Olivetan monk, Matteo Ronto (died, 1443; translation as yet unprinted),[4] by C. d'Aquino (Naples, 1728), by G. Dalla Piazza (Leipzig, 1848), by G. P. Marinelli (Ancona, 1874);

In Polish by A. Stanislawski (Posen, 1870), and by E. Porebowicz (Warsaw, 1899);[5]

---

[1] See also Renier, *Sulla più antica versione francese di Dante*, Turin, 1889 (and regarding this, see J. Camus, in the *Giornale storico della letteratura italiana*, XXXVII, 70 et seq.), and Morel, *Les plus anciennes traductions françaises de la Divine Comédie*, Paris, 1897 (Part I, texts; Part II, notes; and a Supplement by E. Stengel).

[2] On this and other complete German translations, but of less value, see Scartazzini, *Dante in Germania*, II, 192–215; *Giornale dantesco*, I, 183–184; Koch, I, 56–61. We await the completion of a translation by A. Bassermann (cf. *Bullettino della Società dantesca italiana*, N. S., XVI, 145–150).

[3] For other translations in this language, see Kertbeny, *Dante in d. Hungarischen Litteratur*, Berlin, 1873, and the *Bullettino della Società dantesca italiana*, N. S., XV, 160. The *Commedia* has also been translated, wholly or partially, in several Italian dialects. Complete translations are the Ferrarese (1870), the Milanese (1864), and the Venetian (1875).

[4] Of the paraphrase in Latin prose by Gio. da Serravalle we spoke when treating of his commentary (page 117).

[5] The first two canticas of this translation appeared in 1899, but I do not know whether the third has been printed. Likewise I do not know whether any of the Russian translations noted by Koch have been completed.

In Spanish by P. PUIGBÓ (Barcelona, 1870), by M. ARANDA Y
SANJUAN (ibid. 1871), by J. SANCHEZ MORALES (Valencia, 1875;
free translation), by J. DE LA PEZUELA (Madrid, 1879), by D. C.
ROSELL (Barcelona, 1884), by E. DE MONTALBAN (Paris, 1888); [1]

In Swedish by N. LOVÉN (Lund, 1856–1857), by E. LIDFORSS
(Stockholm, 1903), and by T. C. BRING (Upsala, 1906).

VIII

BOOKS AND ARTICLES ON THE FORTUNES OF
THE *COMMEDIA*

A. IN ITALY

G. CARDUCCI, *Della varia fortuna di Dante*, in the volume *Studî
letterarî*, Leghorn, 1874 (and in the eighth volume of the *Opere*,
Bologna, 1893). It is an article well worthy of its author.

L. ROCCA, *Di alcuni commenti della D. C. composti nei primi
vent'anni dopo la morte di Dante*, Florence, 1891.

A. PELLIZZARI, *Il Dittamondo e la Divina Commedia : saggio sulle
fonti del Dittamondo e sull'imitazione dantesca nel secolo XIV*,
Pisa, 1905.

E. CARRARA, *Un oltretomba bucolico*, Bologna, 1899 (these are the
eclogues of Boccaccio inspired by the *Commedia*); A. DOBELLI,
Il culto del Boccaccio per Dante, in the *Giornale dantesco*.

G. MELODIA, *Difesa di Fr. Petrarca*, 2d ed., Florence, 1902 (No. 2
of the *Biblioteca petrarchesca* edited by G. Biagi and G. L. Passerini). It treats of the relations of inspiration and art between
Dante and Petrarch.

V. ROSSI, *Dante e l'umanesimo*, in the volume by various authors,
Con Dante e per Dante, Milan, 1898.

M. BARBI, *La fortuna di Dante nel secolo XVI*, Pisa, 1890 (an
important volume).

---

[1] The oldest Spanish translation is that of Enrico de Villena (first
half of the fifteenth century), as yet unpublished. Cf. M. Schiff, *La
première traduction espagnole de la D. C.*, in the volume in honor of
Menéndez y Pelayo, Madrid, 1899. See also Fr. R. de Uhagón, *Una
traducción castellana desconocida de la D. C.*, Madrid, 1901.

G. B. MARCHESI, *Della fortuna di Dante nel secolo XVII. Appunti*, Bergamo, 1898.

G. ZACCHETTI, *La fama di Dante in Italia nel secolo XVIII. Appunti*, Rome, 1900.

M. ZAMBONI, *La critica dantesca a Verona nella seconda metà del secolo XVIII*, Città di Castello, 1901 (No. 63 of the *Collezione di opuscoli danteschi*).

U. MICOCCI, *Dante nella moderna letteratura italiana e straniera*, Milan, 1893.

V. A. ARULLANI, *Nella scia dantesca : Alcuni oltretomba posteriori alla Divina Commedia*, Alba, 1905.

B. OUTSIDE OF ITALY

G. CHIARINI, *Di una imitazione inglese del Divina Commedia* (the House of Fame by G. Chaucer, the famous English author of the fourteenth century, an imitator of the great Italians of that century), 2d ed., Bari, 1902.[1]

O. KUHNS, Dante and the English Poets from Chaucer to Tennyson, New York, 1904.

P. TOYNBEE, Dante in English Literature from Chaucer to Cary, London, 1909, 2 vols.

E. KOEPPEL, *Dante in d. englischen Litteratur d. XVI*[ten] *Jahrhunderts*, in the *Zeitschrift f. vergleichende Litteraturgeschichte*, N. S., III.

A. VALGIMIGLI, *Il culto di Dante in Inghilterra*, in the *Giornale dantesco*, VI, 1.

A. FARINELLI, *Dante in Francia*, Milan, 1900, 2 vols.[2]

G. A. SCARTAZZINI, *Dante in Germania*. See under "Bibliographies," p. 135.

---

[1] See also the articles on Chaucer therein noted, especially that of Koeppel.

[2] Also by Farinelli see *Dante nelle opere di Christine de Pisan*, in the volume in honor of H. Morf, Halle a/S., 1905, and *Dante e Margherita di Navarra*, in the *Rivista d'Italia* of February, 1902. Hauvette, *Dante nella poesia francese del Rinascimento*, Florence, 1901 (translated from the French. It is No. 36 of the *Biblioteca critica della letteratura italiana*, published by Sansoni).

E. SULGER GEBING, *Dante in d. deutschen Litteratur*, etc., in the *Zeitschrift f. vergleichende Litteraturgeschichte*, Vols. VIII–X (1895–1896).

E. SULGER GEBING, *Goethe und Dante*, Berlin, 1907 (see the full and learned review of this work by A. FARINELLI, in the *Bullettino della Società dantesca italiana*, N. S., XVI, 81–142).

B. SANVISENTI, *I primi influssi di Dante, del Petrarca e del Boccaccio sulla letteratura spagnuola*, Milan, 1902.

A. FARINELLI, *Appunti su Dante in Ispagna nell' età media*, in the *Giornale storico della letteratura italiana*, Suppl. No. 8.

IX

BOOKS IN ENGLISH USEFUL FOR STUDENTS

TRANSLATIONS

(*a*) The Divine Comedy.

H. F. CARY, The Divine Comedy. London. This is published in a cheap edition (the Gladstone), by T. Y. Crowell & Co., New York, with introduction and notes by L. O. Kuhns (and Rossetti's translation of the *Vita nova*). A rather free translation in blank verse, but not in consonance with the latest criticism.

H. W. LONGFELLOW, The Divine Comedy. Boston, Houghton Mifflin Company. A standard literal translation in blank verse, almost word for word, especially valuable for the profuse notes.

JOHN A. CARLYLE, The *Inferno*.

THOMAS OKEY, The *Purgatorio*.

PHILIP H. WICKSTEED, The *Paradiso*.

These three are published in Dent's Temple Classics, with the Italian text and notes by Dr. Oelsner. A most useful edition, offering an opportunity for comparison with the original, with concise but comprehensive notes.

CHARLES E. NORTON, The Divine Comedy. Boston, Houghton Mifflin Company. An exact and scholarly translation, which should be in the hands of every Dante student.

(*b*) The *Vita nova*.

CHARLES E. NORTON, The New Life. Boston, Houghton Mifflin Company. An exact and scholarly translation, rendering the author's thought in precise and literary form.

Dante G. Rossetti, The New Life. Dent's Temple Classics. A poetic and romantic treatment of Dante's work, lacking the faithfulness of Norton.

(c) The *Convivio*.

Philip H. Wicksteed, The *Convivio*. Dent's Temple Classics. A good translation with valuable notes.

(d) Other works.

Latin Works of Dante. Dent's Temple Classics. (*De vulgari eloquentia*, *De monarchia*, Epistles and Eclogues, *Quaestio de aqua et terra*.) Good translations with valuable notes.

(e) The *Canzoniere*.

E. H. Plumptre, The *Canzoniere*. London. Also published by D. C. Heath & Co., Boston, in cheaper form, together with his rhymed translation of the *Commedia*, and a volume of notes and studies.

Dante G. Rossetti, The Early Italian poets. Dent's Temple Classics.

C. H. Grandgent, The *Inferno*. Boston, D. C. Heath & Co. The Italian text, with very full and useful analyses of each canto, and judicious notes. The other two parts are in preparation.

Books of Reference

W. Warren Vernon, Readings on the *Inferno*, *Purgatorio*, and *Paradiso*, 6 vols., London, 1894-1900. (A second and improved edition of this work has appeared.) A valuable book, containing the Italian text, a translation, and an extended discussion.

H. F. Tozer, An English Commentary on Dante's *Divina Commedia*, Oxford, 1901. Most useful.

E. G. Gardner, Dante's Ten Heavens. Westminster and New York, 1900. A study of the *Paradiso*. Important as the only satisfactory treatment in English.

Paget Toynbee, Dictionary of Proper Names and Noteworthy Things in the Works of Dante. Oxford, 1898. Very important. The work of one of the best of English Dantologists.

E. G. GARDNER, Dante. Temple Primers. A necessary handbook for Dante students.

G. A. SCARTAZZINI, A Dante Handbook. Boston, Ginn and Company. A translation by Davidson of this useful and comprehensive but not wholly reliable book.

J. R. LOWELL, Essay on Dante. *In* Among My Books, Vol. II. Boston, Houghton Mifflin Company.

R. W. CHURCH, Dante, and other essays. Macmillan, 1901. The two standard essays on Dante.

A. GASPARY (translated by H. Oelsner), Italian Literature to the Death of Dante. Bohn, 1901. A valuable book.

KARL FEDERN, Dante and his Time. New York, McClure, Phillips & Co., 1902. Very useful, especially for forming an idea of the times.

C. A. DINSMORE, Aids to the Study of Dante. Boston, Houghton Mifflin Company., 1903. A well-chosen compilation of excerpts from the leading Dantologists of all countries. Very useful.

PAGET TOYNBEE, Dante Studies and Researches. London, 1902.

KARL WITTE, Essays on Dante. Boston, Houghton Mifflin Company, 1898.

EDWARD MOORE, Studies in Dante. 3 vols., Oxford, 1896, 1899, 1903. An important series of studies by three authorities. Rather special for the elementary student.

The attention of every Dante student should be called to the three sonnets of Longfellow on the *Commedia*. They are a commentary in themselves, and may be found in his published works and in his translation of Dante.